EDUCATION FOR

PUBLIC RESPONSIBILITY

EDUCATION FOR

PUBLIC RESPONSIBILITY

EDITED AND WITH A PREFACE BY

C. SCOTT FLETCHER, PRESIDENT,

THE FUND FOR ADULT EDUCATION

NEW YORK

W · W · NORTON & COMPANY · INC ·

CONTENTS

v

PREFACE

THIS BOOK is an anthology of speeches made and articles written by Americans during the year 1959. They all deal, in varying degrees of focus, with education, with leadership and with education for leadership. How did they come together as a book? Here is the story.

On April 8, 1959, The Fund for Adult Education announced that it would make awards of $1000 each for the six best speeches or articles on education for public leadership—three for the year 1959, three for the year 1960. This was part of a larger program which the Fund called "Education for Public Responsibility." To those enquiring about these awards (and another category of awards for the best book outlines on executive leadership in the United States), the Fund sent a letter containing the following paragraphs:

"The Awards are designed to generate the best thinking on ways in which more adequate education can be provided to help prepare American leadership on every level of social, economic, and political organization to serve the general welfare.

"For purposes of the Awards, the term "leadership" encompasses the whole range of positions in which executive decision and executive actions have public consequences. It would include, for example, elected and appointed executives in federal, state and municipal governments, corporation executives, members of board of directors of national organizations, school board members and college trustees, foundation officials, labor leaders, leaders of political parties, executives serving abroad, either in government or private positions, et cetera.

"The Fund for Adult Education was established in 1951 by The Ford Foundation as an independent organization having as its central purpose the expansion of opportunities that contribute to the continuing development of the mature individual in the responsible exercise of his freedom, both as a private person and as a citizen. The Fund's special emphasis on preparation for leadership stems from recognizing that the margin of our survival as a free nation depends as never before in our history on the wisdom, courage, and dedication of those responsible for developing and carrying out public policies. It is hoped the Awards will yield insights into such questions as the nature of executive leadership, the ways in which it emerges and is exercised in American society, the major problems which executive leaders face in common, and a kind of education which can best motivate individuals to assume the responsibilities of leadership and best equip them to meet the challenges of the times creatively and with informed devotion to the public welfare."

Interested persons were invited to submit both their own speeches and articles and those of others. The staff of the Fund itself submitted others' speeches and articles they deemed pertinent and worthy. Thousands of magazine articles were read, many of them based upon speeches. Hundreds of "leads" on speeches were followed from newspaper accounts and letters. After December 31, 1959 (the deadline for the awards for that year), nearly 300 documents were in the contest.

A panel of three judges was established. They were:

Chester C. Davis, former government and foundation official;

J. Kenneth Galbraith, Professor of Economics, Harvard University; and

Ordway Tead, Vice President and Editor of Social and Economic Books, Harper & Bros.

A staff committee of the Fund screened the entries and submitted sixteen articles and speeches to the judges. For awards the judges selected the speeches and articles of Emery F. Bacon, Scott Buchanan and F. S. C. Northrop. Excellent as these are, they were judged only according to the specific criteria that the Fund established for its own purposes. Neither the Fund nor the judges would want the ratings to be interpreted as meaningful beyond that point.

This book contains fourteen of the sixteen articles submitted to the judges, including the three prize-winning articles. They are being made available to the general public because they were judged by the Fund and the editors of W. W. Norton & Company to express well important ideas on various aspects of education for responsible self-government.

Probably not one of the submissions was written with the Fund's Award program in mind. All of them touch on the vital theme of education for public responsibility; but more than that, they diffuse light on wider areas of concern, both about education and about the human condition. Read together they illuminate the present state of the American people's adventure with self-government.

The articles and speeches were not selected to illustrate the current national mood. But, come to think of it, they do. And so did the thousands of other articles and speeches which were read during the course of the year. This mood has been variously described as disquiet, alarm, self-examination, dissatisfaction with satisfaction, et cetera. The mood has, since early 1959, taken more definite form in the activity which is now familiar as the "search for national purpose," "the definition of national goals," "the statement (or restatement) of values," "the revaluation of values," and similar phrases.

Self-criticism and self-dissatisfaction are characteristics of the American people, but it seems likely that the present "self-study" is not just another chapter in recurrent appraisal. It has a breadth and an urgency which signify a growing awareness of the need to prepare in unparalleled ways for unparalleled demands.

In the many diagnoses and prescriptions, faith in the power of education, which also is characteristic of America, is pervasive. But here too there are differences. The faith is less doctrinaire. The prescriptions are less glibly written. The nature and process of education are being looked at more searchingly.

The essays in this book are good examples of both diagnoses and prescriptions; they treat both the predicament of the American people today and the education that is called for; they both analyze realities and redefine ideals. They do so from varying vantage points and philosophies, but they share commitment to the values of a self-governing society, concern about its future, and a passionate desire that free men and women continually discover and develop their capacities to the fullest in the responsible use of their freedom both as persons and as citizens.

These articles were written and chosen for purposes other than inclusion in a book. They are the products of powerful, rich and highly developed minds. The question is, how to arrange them? In this volume they are organized into three sections, entitled: "Purpose," "Education" and "Education in Action."

In the first section, "Purpose," Robert M. Hutchins, Adlai Stevenson and Henry Steele Commager consider the requirements which are made of a people who would govern themselves: requirements *from* the nature of self-government and the challenge of other kinds of government; requirements *of* intelligence, morality and dedication. Commager sketches the forces in American society that depress the use of high talent for leadership and the kinds of cultural influences needed to overcome these depressing forces.

In the second section, "Education," the goals, substance and methods of education appropriate for today's and tomorrow's world are treated from three very different points of view. Leo Strauss gives a fresh analysis of the classically liberal theory of learning from the greatest minds. Margaret Mead seeks to add to the "vertical transmission" of learning from the past to the present, from the mature to the immature, a second dimension of "lateral transmission" of the present to the present, of old, middle-aged, young—each to all reciprocally. F. S. C. Northrop gives coherence to the three worlds of politics (free, communist and neutral) and the three worlds of knowledge (the artistic and esthetic, the philosophical and religious, and the logical and scientific).

The final section, "Education in Action," is divided—partly because of its length—into two parts. In the first, "Action Through Society," Henry M. Wriston argues that leadership qualities are unique; that the "utility" of humanists and generalists is great but cannot be measured; and that the development of leaders, humanists and generalists cannot be planned for, but must be encouraged through widespread opportunities for development and expression. Emery F. Bacon considers the responsibility of labor to help individuals achieve excellence as persons and as citizens. Both Arnold H. Maremont and Charles P. Taft counsel that business should stay out of politics *as business*, but that businessmen should participate and encourage others to participate in politics *as citizens*.

In the second part, "Action in Government," four widely different aspects are illuminated. R. G. Cowherd documents Harry Truman's knowledge of American history and how he found in it during hours of need "a perpetual vision of greatness." Harlan Cleveland argues that "bigness" in modern society provides more, rather than fewer, opportunities for participation in decision-making; and that, since more of us take part in the making of decisions with ever-wider consequences, we should prepare ourselves for this role. Henry A. Kissinger analyses the mistakes in conceptions and techniques which obstruct a better use of fine, expertly prepared minds in the making of policy. And in conclusion is Scott Buchanan's thesis that historically our American system of self-government has been a pervasive educational force, that this system has changed to the detriment of our education, and that we may be able to find new ways of learning to govern ourselves by the process of governing ourselves.

C. Scott Fletcher, President
The Fund for Adult Education

ACKNOWLEDGMENTS

EMERY F. BACON, "Achieving Excellence in Labor Education" was an address delivered at the 35th Anniversary of the School for Workers, University of Wisconsin, November 20, 1959. Reprinted by permission of the author.

SCOTT BUCHANAN, "Learning Under Law" was a paper written during 1959 for discussion at a seminar of the National Institute of Mental Health. Reprinted by permission of the author.

HARLAN CLEVELAND, "Dinosaurs and Personal Freedom" appeared in *Saturday Review*, February 28, 1959. Reprinted by permission of *Saturday Review* and the author.

HENRY STEELE COMMAGER, "Urgent Query: Why Do We Lack Statesmen?" was an address delivered at the Massachusetts Institute of Technology, December 3, 1959, and subsequently appeared in *The New York Times Magazine*, January 17, 1960. Reprinted by permission of *The New York Times Magazine* and the author.

R. G. COWHERD, "Mr. Truman's Uses of History" appeared in *The Social Studies*, April, 1959. Reprinted by permission of *The Social Studies* and the author.

ROBERT M. HUTCHINS, "Is Democracy Possible?" was an address delivered on receiving The Sidney Hillman Award for Meritorious Public Service, January 21, 1959. It was subsequently printed in *Saturday Review*, February 21, 1959. Reprinted by permission of the author.

HENRY A. KISSINGER, "The Policymaker and the Intellectual" appeared in *The Reporter*, March 5, 1959. Reprinted by permission of *The Reporter* and the author.

F. S. C. NORTHROP, "What Kind of American Civilization Do We Want?" appeared in *The Annals of The American Academy*, September, 1959. Reprinted by permission of *The Annals of Political and Social Science*, and the author.

ARNOLD H. MAREMONT, "The Dangers of Corporate Activity in Politics" was an address delivered before the Town Hall of Los Angeles, August 4, 1959. Reprinted by permission of the author.

MARGARET MEAD, "A Redefinition of Education" appeared in *NEA Journal*, October, 1959, and grew out of a longer article on the same subject in the *Harvard Business Review*, November–December, 1958. Reprinted by permission of *NEA Journal, Harvard Business Review* and the author.

ADLAI STEVENSON, "Politics and Morality" appeared in *Saturday Review*, February 7, 1959. Copyright 1959 by Adlai E. Stevenson. Reprinted from *Putting First Things First* by Adlai E. Stevenson, by permission of Random House, Inc.

LEO STRAUSS, "What Is Liberal Education?" was an address delivered at the graduation exercises of The Basic Program of Liberal Education for Adults, University College, University of Chicago, June 6, 1959, and published by the University of Chicago Press, June, 1959. Reprinted by permission of the University of Chicago Press and the author.

CHARLES P. TAFT, "Should Business Go In for Politics?" appeared in *The New York Times Magazine*, August 30, 1959. Reprinted by permission of *The New York Times Magazine* and the author.

HENRY M. WRISTON, "Humanists and Generalists" appeared in *The Annals of The American Academy*, September, 1959. Reprinted by permission of *The Annals of Political and Social Science*, and the author.

PURPOSE

IS DEMOCRACY
POSSIBLE? / ROBERT M. HUTCHINS

LAST SATURDAY was the anniversary of an event I have some-times regretted. Sixty years ago last Saturday, on the other side of the East River, near the fire station on Herkimer Street, I was born. My earliest memories of my childhood in Brooklyn are of the horse cars, the ice wagon, the cruller wagon; of yelling git-a-hoss, in the quaint dialect of the region, at an occasional automobile, and playing one-o-cat in front of our house on Dean Street, where we had moved to be near my father's church on the corner of Nostrand and Dean. The faith in which I was brought up was as simple and confident as the environment. Democracy was the answer to everything, including the ills of democracy. These ills would be cured by more democracy. The ideal toward which we were moving was the civilization of the dialogue, where everybody talked with everybody else about everything, where nobody tried to get his way by force or fraud, where everybody was content to abide by the decision of the majority as long as the dialogue could continue. Democracy meant self-government, and self-government meant primarily participation by the individual, at least through the selection of his representatives, in decisions affecting his life and happiness. Since decisions affecting his life and happiness were taken not merely by his government, but also by many other institutions, corporations, trade unions, and politi-cal parties, for example, the thing to do was to democratize them, as well as the government.

In this view the great crime is to try to prevent other people from speaking up, or to say that there are certain things you won't talk about, or certain people you won't talk to, either at home or abroad. In this view education and communication are of prime importance, because if you can't hear what the others are saying, or can't understand it, or if they can't hear or understand you, there can't be any dialogue, and democracy becomes meaningless.

The democratic faith is faith in man, faith in every man, faith that men, if they are well enough educated and well enough informed, can solve the problems raised by their own aggregation.

One advantage of this faith is that it is practically shock-proof. Industrialization can sweep the world. Nationalism and technology can threaten the extinction of the human race. Population can break out all over. Man can take off from this planet as his ancestors took off from the primordial ooze and try to make other planets to shoot from. Education can be trivialized beyond belief. The media of communication can be turned into media of entertainment. The dialogue can almost stop because people have nothing to say, or, if they have something to say, no place to say it. And still it is possible to believe that if democracy and the dialogue can continue, if they can be expanded, if they can be improved, freedom, justice, equality, and peace will ultimately be achieved.

Some shocks I have received lately have bothered me a little. The first came when during the excitement of last year I was recommending my democratic panacea as a remedy for the troubles of the labor unions to the people on the trade union project of the Fund for the Republic. They informed me that the idea of government by the people had little application to labor unions and that in any event democratic forms in unions were no safeguard against anti-social behavior on their part. In fact, they said, some of the unions in which democratic forms were most conspicuous were the most anti-social.

The second shock came when at the conclusion of my usual tirade against the wild irrationality of our foreign policy I explained to the people on the common defense project of the Fund for the Republic that we should subject that policy to democratic control. My colleagues pointed out to me that in addition to being impossible this was unconstitutional, and had always been regarded as such, and that whatever I might think of the policies followed by the President and the Secretary of State, and however much I might dislike being blown up or suffocated as a result of these policies, the Founding Fathers intended that I should be in precisely this position. In any event, they said, there was no way, particularly in view of the enormous technical problems of modern warfare and international relations, in which the citizens could actually participate in the decisions upon which their lives depended.

The third shock came when I was proposing as my usual remedy to the people on the project on political parties, which deals with the political process in a free society. Participation was my watchword. Get out the vote. Or, as the Advertising Council has it, Vote as You Please, but Please Vote. My associates indicated to me that getting people out to vote when they did not know what they were voting for was not helpful, and might be harmful, to the objects I had in view. Under modern conditions, they said, it might be that responsible political participation and decision by the citizens would prove to be impossible, anyway.

Somewhat shaken, I went to the conference on the Island of Rhodes on Representative Government and Public Liberties in the New States. The basic problem of the conference turned out to be whether government by the people is possible, or even desirable, in the modern world. The sense of relief with which members from the new states welcomed military dictatorships in their countries and with which the Frenchmen present welcomed de Gaulle was a measure of the current disenchantment with democracy. These men saw no way of adjusting democratic institutions to contemporary realities. What they hope for is a period of order in which the most acute problems, like Algeria in France and corruption in Siam, may be solved; after which they may, or may not, try government by the people again.

Eminent European philosophers and political scientists present reassured the members from the new states, three of whose governments turned into military dictatorships while the conference was in session, by telling them that democracy was an illusion in both old and new states, for different reasons. In the new states we could not expect government by the people because they lacked education, communication, organization, and law. In the old states

it had been out of date since the Peloponnesian War, and even then
it was not what we mean by democracy now. Pericles, a leader of
the Left, struck thousands of voters from the rolls because they
could not prove that both their parents were native-born Atheni-
ans. Greek democracy was based on a uniformity of ideas and
practices appropriate to an extended family group. The kind of
government by the people that may be said to have worked in
Athens and in the New England town meeting could not possibly
work in a large, heterogeneous, industrial, bureaucratic society.
The most we could hope for was order, efficiency, and the
maintenance of civil liberties, those rights historically carved out
against governmental interference with private life. Alexander
Pope, whose celebrated lines had always seemed to me as false as
they were celebrated, was justified at last:

> For forms of government let fools contest
> Whate'er is best administered is best.

I came away from Rhodes with the foreboding that we might be
at the beginning of something new in the last 100 years—a world-
wide antidemocratic trend that had little or nothing to do with the
intimidations or seductions of the Kremlin. (It was significant that
in eight days of discussion no member from any new state said a
word about Communism or Russia.) This antidemocratic trend
would reverse the aspirations of all men of good will—at least since
1848—for government by the people. It would have alarming
connotations for the United States in the realm of foreign policy.
It should force us to re-examine the assumptions and slogans by
which we have lived in the light of the actual operation of our
institutions in the new industrialized, polarized, bureaucratic
world.

If you ask how my democratic faith is doing,

> Whither is fled the visionary gleam,
> Where is it now, the glory and the dream?

I reply that it is still here. Perhaps the gleam is not quite as bright
as it used to be, and somewhat more visionary, but it is still here.
Yet, even at my age, I cannot long sustain a position to which my
reason will not assent. The shocks I have received are recent; and

I cannot claim that I have absorbed them or that I know how to repel others in the future. Perhaps what I can do is to communicate the sense of crisis that I feel and to ask others to join in thinking for a moment how that faith can be defended.

The faith rests on the propositions that man is a political animal, that participation in political decisions is necessary to his fulfillment and happiness, that all men can and must be sufficiently educated and informed to take part in making these decisions, that protection against arbitrary power, though indispensable, is insufficient to make either free individuals or a free society, that such a society must make positive provisions for its development into a community learning together; for this is what political participation, government by consent, and the civilization of the dialogue all add up to.

If we are to become a community learning together, as I insist we can, the first thing we have to do is to make up our minds that we want to learn. We have lived on a note of triumphant philistinism. Here is a characteristically triumphant proclamation made by Carl D. Becker, perhaps the celebrated American historian of his day, in 1931. He said, "Our supreme object is to measure and master the world, rather than to understand it . . . Viewed scientically, it appears as something to be accepted, something to be manipulated and mastered, something to adjust ourselves to with the least possible stress. So long as we can make efficient use of things, we feel no irresistible need to understand them. No doubt it is for this reason chiefly that the modern mind can be so wonderfully at ease in a mysterious universe."

At ease, indeed! Anybody who feels at ease in the world today is a fool. And anybody who would say now that he was content to master and manipulate the environment without bothering to understand how it worked or what to do with it would show first that he did not know what science was, for science is organized understanding, and second that he had no grasp of the kind of problems we now confront. The great overwhelming problems of our country are how to make democracy a reality, how to survive in the nuclear age, and what to do with ourselves if we do survive. None of these problems is technological, though technology has helped to create all of them, and none of them will yield to the

kind of measurement, manipulation, or mastery that Professor
Becker had in mind. We may, in fact, reverse his statement of 1931
and come nearer the truth of today. Then it would go like this:
no doubt it is because we have felt no irresistible need to understand the world that the modern mind can be so wonderfully ill at
ease in a mysterious universe.

The next question is, how are we going to learn? History will
have trouble with American education in the twentieth century.
It will see a people who say they are dedicated to education and
who are the richest in the world indifferent to education and unwilling to pay for it. It will see an educational system that delivers
less education per dollar than any I can think of saying that all it
needs is more money. The people and the educators are united
only in this: they both want education without pain, either intellectual or financial. History will find it hard to explain how a
nation that *is* one, a nation in which the political subdivisions have
no relation to social or economic life and little to political life,
can entrust its future to these subdivisions by relegating education
to them. History will smile sardonically at the spectacle of this
great country getting interested, slightly and temporarily, in education only because of the technical achievements of Russia, and
then being able to act as a nation only by assimilating education
to the Cold War and calling an education bill a defense act.

We might as well make up our minds to it. If our hopes of
democracy are to be realized, every citizen of this country is going
to have to be educated to the limit of his capacity. And I don't
mean trained, amused, exercised, accommodated, or adjusted. I
mean that his intellectual power must be developed. A good way
to start finding the money that is needed for education would be
to kick out of it the subjects, the activities, and the people that
make no contribution to the development of intellectual power.
Such an operation would produce vast sums.

I suggest that two things might be done with this money and
with any more that may be needed: first, we should double
teachers' salaries, not because all the teachers we have deserve
twice as much as they are getting, but because we want to attract
the ablest people into the profession; and second, we should
establish a national system of scholarships that makes it possible

for every citizen of this country to be educated to the limit of his mental capacity, regardless of the financial capacity of his parents.

If life is learning, and I think it is, and if our object is to become a community learning together, education ought to continue throughout life. Here is the great educational opportunity and obligation of the next generation. The education of adults is not only indispensable to the continuation, expansion, and improvement of the dialogue, but it is also an answer to the question of what we are going to do with ourselves if we survive. As automation advances, as new sources of energy are applied in industry, as the hours of labor decline, we have the chance to become truly human by using our new and disturbing leisure to develop our highest human powers to the utmost. Here we can build on the experience of such organizations as the Great Books Foundation, which has succored tens of thousands of refugees from television.

This brings me to the media of mass communications. If our hopes of democracy are to be realized, the media must supply full and accurate information on which the people can base their judgment on public affairs and they must offer a forum for the discussion of those affairs. I doubt if there are six cities of any size in the United States in which the newspapers come anywhere near meeting these requirements. As for radio and television, with a few distinguished exceptions now and then, they make no attempt to meet them. A dozen years ago the Commission on the Freedom of the Press recommended the establishment of a continuing independent agency, privately financed, to appraise and report periodically on the performance of the media. Everything that has happened since, and especially the use of the most marvelous electronic methods of communication for the communication of the most insignificant material, makes the adoption of this recommendation more urgent every day.

If we were well educated and well informed, could we make ourselves felt in the realm of political action? In the Republic as I have described it every act of assent on the part of the governed is a product of learning. Could we learn by doing in politics? Or would the archaic structure of our government and the vast bureaucratic machine that goes creaking on, following the right procedure instead of seeking the right result, prevent us from using our newly won education and information as active, deciding, responsible citizens?

Today the dialogue is impeded by obsolescent practices and institutions from the long ballot to the presidential primary, from the electoral college to the organization of cities, counties, and states. In too frequent elections unknown persons by the hundreds running for insignificant offices, and improper questions, like the dozens submitted at every California election, are presented to the electorate. This is not democracy, but a perversion of it. The political anatomy is full of vermiform appendices, many of them, like Arkansas, inflamed.

Some of these obsolescent practices stop the dialogue in its tracks, like the failure of the FCC and Congress to develop any concept of the public interest, convenience, and necessity. Some of them distort the dialogue by throwing false weights into it, as the electoral college gives a false weight to the large states and the laws on campaign expenditure give money on overwhelmingly false weight in elections. One thing is certain: if our hopes of democracy are to be realized, the next generation is in for a job of institutional remodeling the like of which has not been seen since the Founding Fathers.

Well, suppose we got this remodeling done. Could we then turn ourselves into active, responsible, participating citizens? Wouldn't the bureaucracy, though better, and administering better laws, still have us by the throat? The answer depends partly on our capacity for political invention, which in 1787 was quite large, and partly on what participation means. If we can be equipped for the dialogue and then invent the means by which the bureaucracy can hear it and be made responsive to it, we shall have come a long way from where we are now in relation, for example, to the State Department and the Atomic Energy Commission. Then political participation would mean not only what it too often means exclusively now, the ballot, but also participation in the dialogue about the ends and means of the political society. We would be a community learning together, and the bureaucracy would be learning, too.

The notion that the sole concern of a free society is the limitation of governmental authority and that that government is best which governs least is certainly archaic. Our object today is not to weaken government in competition with other centers of power, but rather to strengthen it as the agency charged with the responsibility for the common good. That government is best which governs best. Mr. Hoover could see no constitutional way of coping with depression, as Buchanan before him could see no constitutional way of coping with secession. We started out to show in 1932 that our institutions were sufficiently flexible to care for the welfare of all the people. The demonstration was never made. We have got instead the pressure group state, which cares for the welfare of those who are well enough organized to put on the pressure.

The genealogy of this development is strange. When I was a boy, we knew what stood between us and freedom, justice, and equality: it was special privilege. Get rid of special privilege, we said, and the common good will be achieved. In our time pacification has been attained not by getting rid of special privilege but by extending it, by extending it to those well enough organized to threaten the special privileges under attack.

Is the tariff hurting the farmers? Retain the tariff and subsidize the farmers. Are administered prices hurting labor? Let's have administered wages, too. Is industry demoralized by expense accounts and tax dodges? Let's have featherbedding in labor, too. Is something done by some group anti-social? Let's all of us—all of us who can put on the pressure—be anti-social, too. And if a federal agency is established to regulate us, never fear: we have the pressure that will shortly make the agency the servant and mouthpiece of the interests it was intended to control. And as we laughingly count our gains at the expense of the public, we can reverently repeat the solemn incantation that helped to make them possible: that government is best which governs least.

The Constitution must protect the citizen against the government. The government must protect him against society and the rapacity of organizations in it by seeing to it that these organizations pursue purposes and program consonant with the common good.

The stresses and strains in our society are obscured for us partly by our preoccupation with Russia, which plays a curious double role as the devil in our world and as the standard by which we measure our progress. If we weren't getting ahead of Russia, or falling behind her, how could we tell where we were?

Our real problems are also concealed from us by our current remarkable prosperity, which results in part from the production of arms that we do not expect to use, and in part from our new way of getting rich, which is to buy things from one another that we do not want at prices we cannot pay on terms we cannot meet because of advertising we do not believe.

But beneath these superficial manifestations, beneath our fantasies of fear on the one hand and wealth on the other, are moving those great, fundamental, historic forces which will put our institutions and our democratic faith to the test. This is the basic fact of our life as a people.

I have never subscribed to the proposition once debated in the Oxford Union, that in the opinion of this House Columbus went too far. Nor can I bring myself to refer to man, as he is now referred to in military technology, as a "biomechanical link." If Columbus had not gone so far, man might never have had the chance to become anything more than a biomechanical link. America is still the hope of mankind. It is still our responsibility, now more than ever, to see to it that government of the people, by the people, and for the people does not perish from the earth.

POLITICS AND MORALITY / ADLAI STEVENSON

ALL POLITICS is made up of many things—economic pressures, personal ambitions, the desire to exercise power, the overriding issues of national need and aspiration. But if it is nothing more, it is without roots. It is built on shifting, changing sands of emotion and interest. When challenged, it can give no account of itself. When threatened, it is in danger of collapse.

Today, when the threat and challenge to free society seem more total and powerful than ever before, it is not a political luxury or fruitless pedantry to re-examine our fundamental principles. I think it more likely to be the condition of survival.

There comes to mind a phrase of the late A. Powell Davies, whose ministry in Washington was a national beacon for so many years. "The world," he said, "is now too dangerous for anything but the truth, too small for anything but brotherhood." This I believe to be in broad measure a correct estimate of the condition of human society, which is now capable, with a few hydrogen bombs, of extinguishing itself. Today we can all be killed by the same bombs or atomic fallout. In that sense we have a desperate physical solidarity. But moral and social solidarity in the family of man is still to be found.

Not so long ago I visited Dr. Albert Schweitzer in his primitive jungle hospital in French Equatorial Africa, and he told me he considered this the most dangerous period in history, not just modern history, but all human history. Why? Because, he said, heretofore nature has controlled man, but now man has learned to

control elemental forces—before he has learned to control himself.

Many of us seem to rely on some mythical God-given superi-
ority of the white Western world to save us. My concern is that
there is evidence that the Communists accept the reality of the
human condition more than we do.

It is impossible to spend weeks traveling around the Soviet
Union as I did without taking away an overwhelming impression
of thrust and purpose in most aspects of Soviet life. The revolutionary ardor has cooled with time, but even the very pragmatic
political leaders seem to believe profoundly in the truth of their
way of life, and there are quietly confident that it will sweep the
world in time. I think they sincerely believe that their methods,
their aspirations, their dreams, make up the final truth about the
nature of man and society.

From this conviction flow two consequences. The first is that
no effort, no dedication, no sacrifice is too great that may help to
realize the Communist Party's goals in Soviet society. The second
is that no corner of humanity can be a matter of indifference to
the Communists because the whole human race is destined to become one in Communist brotherhood.

These are not abstract generalizations. The Soviet Union is a
vast powerhouse of energy all harnessed to the communal task of
building the Soviet dream. The thrust of economic growth that
adds a 9 or 10 per cent increase each year to industrial expansion
is one aspect of this energy. The vast sums available for science
and research are another. The self-discipline and long hours put in
by school children to train themselves as the scientists, technicians,
considered this the most dangerous period in history, not just
administrators, and linguists of the new world order are perhaps
the most significant measure of the resources of energy, work and
skill upon which Soviet leaders hope to draw. In Moscow, Serge
Obraztsov, the brilliant director of the famous Puppet Theatre,
said: "I visited China five years ago. It was the most extraordinary
experience of my life. People in China have had nothing—nothing!
Now several hundred million people are dreaming of tomorrow.
I cannot describe to you the feeling of excitement there—much,
much more even than here in the Soviet Union."

The energy, the drive, the dedication in the U.S.S.R. spill over into international affairs. In part, of course, this is the restless concern that all imperial powers must exercise, especially when the peoples they control are as restive and unreliable as the captive peoples in Russia's European empire. But Communist activity, planning, and efforts in trade and aid are not confined to areas of Communist control. They are world-wide, and there is no corner of the earth's surface that they think too insignificant for their attention. But why should they be so busy? Why such patience through every setback, such forward thrusts through every point of Western weakness? Heaven knows, we only want to stay home. Why don't they? Why do we never meet an isolationist Communist?

I don't think there is any doubt about the answer. Part of it is simply needed foreign trade. Part is fear—the search for security through friends. And part is the historical centrifugal forces in Russia that have been pressing outward for a hundred years—to the Pacific, the Balkans, and the Middle East. But the important thing is that the Soviet Russians believe in their truth, as the men of the Western world once believed in theirs. They, not we, are firing the shots that are heard round the world—and also the satellites that orbit above it. The fact that their faith is in many ways an evil perversion of the great propositions that once made the blood course in our Western veins does not alter the fact that their tempo is dynamic and ours sluggish—even, I think, to ourselves.

The reason cannot be that we Americans have lost our vision of truth and brotherhood. No country on earth owes the sense of community more explicitly to the fact that it is united not by race or nationality but by fidelity to an idea. We were born "dedicated to a proposition" and our greatest leaders—the Jeffersons, the Lincolns, the Woodrow Wilsons—were not great because they achieved purely American purposes, but because they were able to speak for humanity at large and extended their vision to the whole family of man.

Nor, I believe, can we find fault with the American dream. Indeed, the ferment of our freedom works inexorably and dangerously in the Communist world. No one can have visited Poland without seeing how little the Polish people accept their servitude and how they look beyond their neighbors to the free world as the reservoir of power and hope.

But, alas, all our talk—in diplomacy, in strategy, in aid and trade, in all the intricacies of our world-wide relations—has been to a depressing degree purely defensive. We have offered aid—not to help others but to shield ourselves. We have reacted to countless Soviet initiatives; acted on our own initiative barely at all. We watch the skies for other people's sputniks and listen to the telegraph wires for other people's moves. Yet we are the free men of this universe, the children of liberty, the beneficiaries of unequalled abundance, and heirs of the highest, proudest political tradition ever known to man!

Why this lack of initiative? Why this paralysis of will? What have we done to our truth and our brotherhood—the supreme truth of freedom, the Christian truth of brotherly love? Have they failed or have we?

There is no more urgent duty than to discover why we have failed and to get back into the arena, aspiring, striving, fighting once more for what we believe. I am not basically worried about our technology, our science, our machines, our resources. But I am concerned, desperately concerned, about the enfeebled great central pulse of our freedom, the great truth of liberty, which, more than any other nation, we first set working in the modern world.

The great German poet, Goethe, who also lived through a crisis of freedom, said to his generation: "What you have inherited from your fathers, earn over again for yourselves or it will not be yours." We inherited freedom. We seem unaware that freedom has to be remade and re-earned in each generation of man. One reason for this failure is, I believe, passing at last. Our foolish languor has been shaken, if not shattered. We are more ready to examine ourselves and our record. And it is a privilege of our society that every citizen should make his own inquiry. The urgent thing is to feel the need for rethinking and to set to work the ultimate energies of free society—which cannot be done by the fiat of government but only by the troubled conscience of responsible men and women.

I believe that we have confused the free with the free and easy.

If freedom had been the happy, simple, relaxed state of ordinary humanity, man would have everywhere been free—whereas through most of time and space he has been in chains. The natural government of man is servitude. Tyranny is the normal pattern of government. It is only by intense thought, by great effort, by burning idealism, and unlimited sacrifice that freedom has prevailed as a system of government. And the efforts that were first necessary to create it are fully as necessary to sustain it in our own day.

He who offers this thing we call freedom as the soft option is a deceiver or himself deceived. He who sells it cheap or offers it as the byproduct of this or that economic system is knave or fool. For freedom demands infinitely more care and devotion than any other political system. It puts consent and personal initiative in the place of command and obedience. By relying upon the devotion and initiative of ordinary citizens, it gives up the harsh but effective disciplines that underpin all the tyrannies which over the millennia have stunted the full stature of men.

We have had enough of adjustment, conformity, easy options, and the least common denominator in our system. We need instead to see the "pursuit of happiness" in terms that are historically proven and psychologically correct. If we become a nation of Bourbons, numbers won't save us. We shall go their way.

This is not a Puritan or pleasure-hating spirit. On the contrary, there is no boredom or misery to equal the pursuit of distraction alone. We do not slip into happiness. It is strenuously sought and earned. A nation glued to the television screen is not simply at a loss before the iron pioneers of the new collective society. It isn't even having a good time. No society has ever spent so much as we do on drink and tranquilizers. Can one argue that this is evidence of universal fun?

But perhaps this misunderstanding of the true nature of happiness and of the conditions of its pursuit is simply an aspect of something else—our misunderstanding of the real nature of freedom. Judge Learned Hand has warned us that freedom would not survive in our Constitution if it had already died in the hearts of the people. We shall not have a free society unless we have free men.

How are we to defend freedom if, for the tyranny of external control, we substitute the clattering, cluttering tyranny of internal aimlessness and fuss? This freedom for our souls, freedom at the profoundest level of our being, is not a gift to us by our contemporary way of life. On the contrary, much of this life is a direct conspiracy against it. And if we cannot—by a certain discipline, by readiness for reflection and quiet, by determination to do the difficult and aim at a lasting good—rediscover the real purpose and direction of our existence, we shall not be free. Our society will not be free.

I doubt if any society in history has faced so great a moral challenge as ours, or needed more desperately to draw on the deepest sources of courage and responsibility. Ours is the first human community in which resources are so abundant that almost no policies lie beyond our capacity for purely physical reasons. The inhibitions of poverty—lack of resources, lack of capital, lack of power—do not hold us back. We can accomplish what we aim at. Thus, perhaps for the first time in the world, choice not means, ends not instruments, are decisive.

Then again we have proved—drably and dangerously—over the last decade that defensiveness is not a sufficient reason for action. All the policies we have pursued in self-defense have left us still on the defensive. But if we do not act from fear, we must find some other motivation. In free society there is no other alternative but to tap the vigor, faith, and imagination of the people themselves.

But perhaps the most urgent reason why the quality of our moral response has become the decisive issue in politics is quite simply that most of the major problems of our day present themselves in moral terms, and are probably insoluble without some stirring of generosity, some measure of vision. In the wealthiest nation in the world, at least 5,000,000 families still live in squalid but remediable poverty. They are a minority. They don't have the votes to force the issue of their misfortune into the front rank of public issues. They depend, for remedies, upon the alert conscience of the majority. But how do we keep the conscience sensitive and alert? By concentrating on our own concerns and adding the dishwasher to the television set to the air conditioner? By griping over taxes? By closing our minds every time we go through a slum? No—we shall have the dedication and drive to wipe poverty out of his rich land only if the well-to-do majority of today do not repeat the selfish indifference which, in many communities, has been the epitaph of yesterday's wealthy elite.

The issue of the rights and status of our colored citizens is our small share of a world-wide problem. The four hundred years' dominance of men of white skin is ending. The vast colored majority of mankind is seeking the opportunity and the respect that white people have been lucky enough to enjoy for so long—sometimes at the colored people's expense. But, within this world-wide crisis, we in America, with our colored minority, have a major role to play—for good or evil. "The unfinished work" that Lincoln left us, of creating a society in which all men can hold up their heads as equals and self-respecting citizens, can never be accomplished unless there are enough white men and women who resist in the core of their being the moral evil of treating any of God's children as essentially inferior.

Nor is this simply a question of our own national community. It is a painful fact that the Communists show a world-wide concern, which is largely lacking among the men of the West; the whole human race is their horizon. Their "brotherhood" is materialist, collectivist, atheist, and we dislike it, but it embraces everybody, and it is the framework of policies that takes the missionaries of their new order to the ends of the earth. We have no corresponding commitment to our fellowmen. For hundreds of years, we have preached the Christian promise of brotherhood, but today, when vanishing space and scientific revolution have turned our planet into a single neighborhood, the ideal means little in terms of concern or conviction, in terms of policy or action.

Here we are in the Atlantic world, 16 per cent of the world's peoples consuming 70 per cent of the world's wealth. We cannot be indifferent to the moral implications of this gap. I do not know how we can gain a new perspective about the narrow world of plenty and poverty in which we live unless moral insights of justice and compassion stir us to understand the privileged position in which we live.

This age has been defined in many ways—as a time of conflict in ideology, as a time of ferment in technology, as a period of revolution in science, as an era when at last the means lie at hand to free mankind from the ancient shackles of pain, and hunger. It is all these things—but I believe the true crisis of our times lies at a deeper level. All this freedom and elbow room only thrusts onto us with more force the fundamental issue of the faith that is in us. We can use our wealth and capacity for some vision of truth, some ideal of brotherhood, or we can imprison ourselves within the selfishness of our own concerns and the limitations of a narrow nationhood.

One may argue that these qualities—of dedication and selfishness—are remote from the realities of politics. They are all very well for private life, but what part can they play in the rough and tumble of partisanship, of primaries, conventions, and election campaigns? Ambition, drive, material interests, political skills, the art of maneuver—all these, one might say, have their part, but do not let us pretend that the democratic process is primarily a school of virtue or an arena of moral combat.

It has been the view of great philosophers and great statesmen that our system of free government depends in the first instance upon the virtue of its citizens. Montesquieu made virtue the condition of republican government. Washington declared that it could not survive without it. We have had 175 years of it since their time and no one can deny that the system has survived a remarkable amount of skulduggery. In fact, it is probably a tougher system than its founders imagined. For no democratic system can survive without at least a large and active leaven of citizens in whom dedication and selflessness are not confined to private life, but are the fundamental principles of their activity in the public sphere.

Naked interest and naked ambition will carry a lot of people naturally and inevitably into politics. We do not need societies for the promotion of lobbies; interests, good and bad, will promote themselves. Nor, in any generation, do we lack politicians whose only principle of action is the advancement of their own career—the starry-eyed opportunists, and all the other eager men in a hurry to the top.

There has never been any disinterested reform without disinterested reformers. And here we come to the essential contribution made by dedication and selflessness to the public good. No one ever did any good in politics without readiness for endless hard work—for the grinding, boring, tedious work, as well as the glamorous, high-sounding, headline-hitting work. No reforms come easy; even the most obvious will have its entrenched enemies. Each one is carried to us on the bent and weary backs of patient, dedicated men and women.

They are not only dedicated in their readiness to give energy and hard work to the cause; they must also have sufficiently clear sight and open minds and hearts to see the need for reform in the first place. But clear sight and an open heart for others' needs is again something that hardly "comes naturally." We have so many needs of our own—our families, our jobs, our homes, and fortunes, our prospects. We are hemmed in with needs and interests, weighty, urgent, honorable human needs and interests, even if they are exclusively our own. It takes an extra dimension of vision to see beyond our inner circle of interest. Most people, most of the time, do not possess it—which is one reason why self-regarding interests make up so much of the stuff of politics. And this is why the men and women of genuine, imperturbable public spirit seem so few and far between.

There is a danger of this element of vision vanishing almost wholly from our political life. In the main we are so comfortable; so many evils of the past have shrunk in size and almost out of sight.

When the multitudes gathered, a hundred years ago, to listen in rapt attention for hours to the Lincoln-Douglas debates, had they fewer responsibilities and duties than the citizens of today to many of whom the great issues of politics seem to be most usefully conveyed in fifteen-second television flashes of subliminal advertising?

It is not possible that the pressures of personal responsibilities are not greater but that the dedication and selflessness needed to discern and influence public issues have shrunk? In a century in which so many of the mentors of the public mind—from the psychiatrists to the ad-men—speak to us in terms of "what we owe to ourselves," may there not indeed have been a slackening of devotion as compared with those days, not so long distant, when what man owes to God and his neighbor was a common theme of public discourse?

If so, this is a dangerous hour for our politics and for government by consent of the governed. For at no time have so many of the great issues of the day demanded clear, real moral vision to bring them into focus.

URGENT QUERY: WHY DO WE LACK
STATESMEN? / *HENRY STEELE COMMAGER*

THE UNITED STATES of the Seventeen Seventies and Eighties was a new nation on the frontier of civilization, with a population of some three million (far less than that of Los Angeles County today) spread thin over an immense territory, without a single real city, without an aristocracy or a ruling class, and with few of those institutions of science and learning that sustained the societies of the Old World. Yet out of this America emerged, in a single generation, Washington, Franklin, Jefferson, Hamilton, John Adams, James Wilson, John Jay, James Madison, John Marshall and a score of others scarcely less distinguished in the realm of statesmanship.

Now we have everything that we then lacked. Our population is fifty times as large as that of 1780, our territory spreads across the continent, we count a hundred cities larger than the largest of that time, we boast an educational level higher than any other in the Western world, as well as immense wealth and power. We have, in fact, all the elements that should produce statesmen. Yet in the past half century we have produced perhaps three men comparable to those of the Revolutionary generation: Theodore Roosevelt, Woodrow Wilson and Franklin Roosevelt (some would add Adlai Stevenson but he is as yet untried).

Indeed, the most conspicuous feature on the American political landscape is the absence of statesmanship.

Nor is this a matter of individuals or of personalities; if so, our analysis might well be suspect. If we look away from the great figures of history to the principles they formulate, the contrast between the Revolutionary generation and our own is even more striking. The generation of the Founding Fathers invented—or perfected—almost all of our major political institutions: the federal system, the constitutional convention, the written constitution, a new system that did away with the colony-mother country relationship, a system of checks and balances that really checked and balanced, and even the modern political party.

What has the twentieth century invented, in the realm of politics? Two things, perhaps, that can bear comparison with the great institutions of the past: the concept of regional development crystallized in T.V.A., and the Marshall Plan. But both of these, important as they are, are chiefly administrative contrivances rather than political institutions. The fact is that for a century and a half we have been living on the political capital piled up by the generation of the Founding Fathers and have added little to it.

How explain what appears to be a precipitous decline in statesmanship? Why is it that a nation so great and a people so fertile in so many fields are so unproductive in this field of such paramount importance?

It is not easy to answer questions of this kind, for we do not know what accounts for greatness. How, after all, explain the outburst of genius in the Athens of Pericles and Sophocles, the Florence of Michelangelo and Raphael, the England of Hakluyt and Shakespeare, the Copenhagen of Hans Anderson and Kierkegaard and Thorvaldsen, the Vienna of Haydn and Mozart and Beethoven?

It would be absurd to ascribe all these to coincidence or to chance. Sculptors and painters didn't just happen in fifteenth-century Florence, nor navigators and poets and dramatists in the little England of Elizabeth; nor was it chance that frontier Virginia, with a white population less than that of Knoxville or Syracuse, gave us Washington, Jefferson, George Mason, John Marshall, James Madison, George Wythe and a dozen others of distinction. Perhaps if we can find out why art was the specialty of Florence and Venice, music of Salzburg and Vienna, and statesmanship of Revolutionary Virginia, we can find some ex-

planation of the decline of statesmanship in our own day, and
some clue to the secret of its revival.

The most obvious consideration is that of contingency. Talent
is infectious, even genius is infectious. In a society where everybody is interested in art, where artists are the objects of admiration and of patronage, where the visible achievements of the
artists confront one at every turn, every boy will want to wield
a painter's brush or a stonecutter's chisel. In a society where to
be ignorant of music is to be ignorant of life, the most natural
thing is to learn to sing, to play a fiddle or a pianoforte. A society
where to sail in the service of the Queen is the highest honor,
where all the talk is of new lands and new oceans, is one that almost inevitably produces Drakes and Frobishers and Raleighs.

What is decisive, in each case, is the standard of excellence
and of patronage or—to use the current idom—of prestige. And
a society where lawyers argue political principles before the jury,
where parsons expound them from their pulpits, and judges from
the bench, where the talk is everywhere of great political issues,
is one where everyone of talent naturally gravitates to the public
service.

For the young are creatures of contingency. They pattern
their lives on the standards which their society in fact (not in
theory) exalts. They will adopt standards that are held up to
them, but only on the condition that these are genuine standards,
only on condition that their elders do subscribe to them and live
by them, in deed as in word. Thus, as Pericles asserted, they
"draw strength not from twice-told arguments * * * but from the
busy spectacle of our great city's life, as we have it before us
day by day, falling in love with her as we see her."

What is that "busy spectacle" which our young see before
them day by day, from which they are to draw inspiration? What
are the things we most admire and most generously reward? And
let us not ask what is said in commencement addresses or at Fourth
of July celebrations, what is earnestly argued in unread editorials
or in the solemn articles sandwiched between the advertising
matter in the popular magazines, what is expounded on the
"public service" programs of television and radio. Let us ask rather
what it is the newspapers put in their headlines; what programs are

assigned the choice spots on radio and television; what aspects of school life really command the enthusiasm of the public?

If we ask what our young people are expected to admire and to emulate, the answer is easy enough. It is private enterprise. The great rewards in our society go to the leaders of business, industry and finance. It is the business men, the bankers, the corporation executives, who run their communities. They are the men who sit on the boards of the universities, the hospitals, the orchestras and the museums; they are the men who garner the richest harvest of honorary degrees from universities whose business is presumably scholarship.

They are the men President Eisenhower appoints to Cabinet or ambassadorial posts, puts on committees—even on committees dealing with education or with science—and invites to his important White House dinners. As the specialty of eighteenth-century Virginia and Massachusetts was statesmen, our specialty is business men and technicians.

"What is honored in a country will be cultivated there," said Plato. We are reminded, too, of the proud boast of Pericles:

"Our citizens attend both to public and private duties, and do not allow absorption in their own affairs to interfere with their knowledge of the city's."

Washington might have made the same boast, and Jefferson, but how many can make it now?

There are a number of reasons for this:

Consider first the connotations of the terms involved. The term "private enterprise" has glamour; the term "public enterprise" is dull and prosaic. Day in and day out, in a thousand media, private enterprise is equated with the American way of life. It is "private enterprise" that has made us what we are. It is "private enterprise" that most sharply distinguishes us from the Communists. It is "private enterprise" that will save us. One of our major political parties poses as peculiarly the spokesman and champion of private enterprise, and its two titular leaders never cease to extol that concept, or to throw suspicion on the alternative. Witness the attitude toward the T.V.A. or public housing or socialized medicine!

School boards enjoin teachers to indoctrinate students with the glories of private enterprise, and textbooks are required to celebrate its virtues. The man who devotes himself to private enterprise is looked upon as a public benefactor.

Public enterprise, by contrast, is either tiresome or suspect. The label "politician" is one of opprobrium and, since Senator McCarthy's crusade, a faint aura of suspicion hangs over the term "civil servant" as well. The head of a business firm is an executive, but the head of a government office is a bureaucrat.

As for public enterprise itself, it conjures up such images as public housing, federal dams and hydroelectric power and public health programs. To many minds these have the taint of socialism which, as everyone knows, is next door to communism. Certainly, if we hearken to some of our medical spokesmen, a plan for national health which enlists the government in the enterprise is a plot hatched in Moscow.

It is natural enough that with this attitude we reward private service much more generously than public—not only in money but in respect and prestige as well. The contrast between the pay of the Supreme Court justice and the corporation lawyer, the T.V.A. engineer and the engineer of the private power company, the scientist in the Public Health Service and the surgeon in private practice, is too familiar to rehearse; it is not, perhaps, of central importance.

More important are the conditions of private and public service. Not only is public service badly paid; it is exceedingly vulnerable, and more so now than at any time in the past. It was Horace Greeley who observed bitterly during the campaign of 1872 that he didn't know whether he was running for the Presidency or the penitentiary. A good many politicians, and not Presidential candidates alone, must have felt that way during some of our recent campaigns—the "twenty years of treason" type of campaign, for example.

The civil servant, too, is at all times fair game: fair game for demagogues making political capital; for Congressional committees which allow themselves a degree of irresponsibility unparalled in other English-speaking countries; for security investigators whose work—witness the Service and the Condon cases—is never done; even for newspaper men who yield nothing to these investigators in their contempt for privacy.

Another reason we are short on statesmen is that we no longer train for service to the commonwealth as did the generation of the Founding Fathers. At no time, to be sure, has there been more provision for *formal* training: Syracuse, Tufts, Harvard, Princeton, American and many other universities maintain flourishing institutes for the study of public administration or the foreign service. But valuable as this training is, it comes too late, and in a form too academic. The time to excite the imagination and stir the sympathies is in early youth, and the place is in the home and the community.

Thus the patriot Josiah Quincy left to his son "the Works of Algernon Sidney, John Locke, Bacon, Gordon's Tacitus, and Cato's Letters when he should have reached the age of 15" that he might be trained to the love of liberty. Thus George Mason —author of the great Virginia Declaration of Rights—charged his children "on a father's blessing, never to let the motives of private interest or of ambition induce them to betray nor the fear of danger or death deter them from asserting the liberty of the country and endeavoring to transmit to their posterity those sacred rights to which they themselves were born."

This attitude of the eighteenth century suggests another explanation of the decline of statesmanship in our time—the decline not only of the study of history but of the study of history in terms of great men and heroic enterprises.

The generation that won independence and created a nation was deeply versed in the history of Greece and of Rome, the history of Switzerland, of the Low Countries, and of England— which is another way of saying the history of freedom. They were familiar with Thucydides and Plutarch and with Milton and John Locke; they thought of themselves as part of a great tradition and immersed themselves in that tradition in order to perpetuate it.

We study history, to be sure, but in terms of impersonal "forces" or, worse yet, in accordance with the Headache Theory that history is just one "problem" after another. And when we teach it in the schools (we have to "require" it) we manage to drain it of heroes and heroics and reduce it to a drab level guaranteed to frustrate interest and smother imagination.

"After history has done its best to fix men's thoughts upon

strategy and finance," said Justice Holmes, "their eyes have
turned and rested on some single romantic figure—some Sidney,
some Falkland, some Wolfe, some Montcalm. * * * This is that
little touch of the superfluous which serves no mechanical end.
Superfluous only as glory is superfluous, or a bit of red ribbon
that a man would die to win." To which we may remark, "Not if
our schools can help it!"

Somewhere, too, we have lost that passionate concern for the
future that animated the generation of Washington and Jefferson,
that sense of responsibility to "our descendants to the thousandth
and thousandth generation" to which Jefferson referred so mov-
ingly in his inaugural address. We have lost not only the eighteenth-century faith in progress, but Victorian optimism as well;
few of us really think the best is yet to be, the last for which
the first was made. We want the best to be now, and we want
to enjoy it ourselves.

We may believe in a future where airplanes fly twice as fast
and all drudgery is eliminated by gadgets, but we do not believe in
a future which will unveil comparable advances in the moral or
cultural realms.

The generation of the Founding Fathers was extroardinarily
conscious of posterity. As John Adams wrote of the signing of
the Declaration:

"Through all the gloom I can see the rays of ravishing light and
glory. Posterity will triumph in that day's transaction."

In a curious way, we no longer believe in posterity; perhaps we
no longer believe in the young. We do not, for example, believe
enough in posterity to save the forests, the soil, the water and
other natural resources as fiduciaries for future generations. It
may even be questioned whether we believe in posterity enough
to persuade us to small efforts or small sacrifices. The nineteenth
century could support a "St. Nicholas" and a "Youth's Com-
panion"; we fob our young people off with television programs in-
culcating violence and sadism.

The nineteenth century permitted the young to keep their
games and sports for their own enjoyment; we professionalize
even school sports for the entertainment and profit of adults.
Domestic architecture, that almost infallible index of a people's
philosophy, proclaims our indifference to the claims of children.

The nineteenth century could afford to build houses with nurseries, verandas for rainy days, attics and lumber rooms for play, even with rooms for books and a piano. We build more expensive and more hygienic houses with no room for privacy or for play.

Other people, more concerned with the health of their children, can afford bicycle paths; we drive children off the roads with our giant cars. Other people, poorer than we, can afford parks and squares in their great cities; we take all available space for parking lots.

We can submit this attitude toward posterity to another and simpler test: the Founding Fathers, for all their misgivings about democracy, wrote no limitations on the expression of the popular will into the Constitution. It has remained for our generation to provide a massive vote of no-confidence in the political judgment of the future: by the Twenty-second Amendment we substitute *our* judgment for theirs on the crucial matter of electing a President.

Two final considerations illuminate the problem of statesmanship, particularly in the last quarter of a century—the emergence in the United States of a patriotism that is narrow and chauvinistic, and the growth of statism.

The men who won our independence and laid the foundations of the American nation were devoted patriots but they were, too, men of the world. For all their devotion to the nation they were creating, they were children of the Enlightenment. Reason taught them that all men were brothers, that purely national distinctions were artificial, and that there existed a great community of art and letters and philosophy and science cutting across and transcending mere national boundaries. The Declaration of Independence, it is relevant to recall, appealed to the opinion of Mankind, and asserted the Rights of Man.

The nationalism of the eighteenth century, then, did not rest on a narrow base but on a broad one. It was not exclusive but inclusive. It did not find nourishment in fear and suspicion, or in hatred—as so much of our current patriotism does—but in faith and confidence. Perhaps one reason for the decline in statesmanship is that we have hemmed our potential statesmen in, we have denied them, as it were, tolerant and spacious ideas.

This has had two deplorable consequences. In the first place, it has put a premium on ostentatious displays of chauvinism, and discouraged patriotism that is high-minded and disinterested. A kind of Gresham's Law has set in in the realm of public policy, bogus patriotism driving out the real thing, rhetoric supplanting eloquence, lip service substituting for true loyalty.

In the second place, it has steadily narrowed the concept and constricted the practice of genuine statesmanship. For years now the test of statesmanship has not been broad horizons, catholic sympathies, spacious ideas, but energetic hostility to communism or to ideas that some might think subversive.

This is not the way to foster love of country and service to her; it is rather the way to create a shabby concept both of love and of country, and to turn service into disservice.

The same cast of mind and the same pressures that have encouraged chauvinistic nationalism have stimulated the growth of statism. Its emergence can be most clearly seen in the new doctrines that require travel to be "in the best interests of the United States"; that regard the gathering of information about a foreign country as a "function of the conduct of foreign policy"; that subordinate the rights of freedom of speech, of the press, of association, to Congressional notions of what is in the "national interest"; that take away even the citizenship of a native-born American if Congress thinks his conduct interferes with the conduct of foreign policy.

In a hundred other ways, too, we are enhancing the power of the state—making science, education, art and letters handmaidens to the state. Nothing will more surely dry up the wellsprings of a genuine patriotism than the creation of a *mystique* of the state. All those who think it appropriate to subordinate the interests of freedom to the supposed interests of the state should heed the admonition of John Stuart Mill:

"A state which dwarfs its men, in order that they may be more docile instruments in its hands even for beneficial purposes will find that with small men no great thing can really be accomplished."

EDUCATION

WHAT IS LIBERAL EDUCATION? / *LEO STRAUSS*

YOU HAVE acquired a liberal education. I congratulate you on your achievement. If I were entitled to do so, I would praise you for your achievement. But I would be untrue to the obligation which I have undertaken if I did not supplement my congratulations with a warning. The liberal education which you have acquired will avert the danger that the warning will be understood as a counsel of despair.

Liberal education is education in culture or toward culture. The finished product of a liberal education is a cultured human being. "Culture" (*cultura*) means primarily agriculture: the cultivation of the soil and its products, taking care of the soil, improving the soil in accordance with its nature. "Culture" means derivatively and today chiefly the cultivation of the mind, the taking care and improving of the native faculties of the mind in accordance with the nature of the mind. Just as the soil needs cultivators of the soil, the mind needs teachers. But teachers are not as easy to come by as farmers. The teachers themselves are pupils and must be pupils. But there cannot be an infinite regress: ultimately there must be teachers who are not in turn pupils. Those teachers who are not in turn pupils are the great minds or, in order to avoid any ambiguity in a matter of such importance, the greatest minds. Such men are extremely rare. We are not likely to meet any of them in any classroom. We are not likely to meet any of them anywhere. It is a piece of good luck if there is a single one alive in one's time. For all practical purposes, pupils, of whatever degree of proficiency, have access to the teachers who are not in turn pupils, to the greatest minds, only through the great books. Liberal education will then consist in studying with the proper care the great books which the greatest minds have left behind—a study in which the more experienced pupils assist the less experienced pupils, including the beginners.

This is not an easy task, as would appear if we were to consider the formula which I have just mentioned. That formula requires a long commentary. Many lives have been spent and may still be spent in writing such commentaries. For instance, what is meant by the remark that the great books should be studied "with the proper care"? At present I mention only one difficulty which is obvious to everyone among you: the greatest minds do not all tell us the same things regarding the most important themes; the community of the greatest minds is rent by discord and even by various kinds of discord. Whatever further consequences this may entail, it certainly entails the consequence that liberal education cannot be simply indoctrination. I mention yet another difficulty. "Liberal education is education in culture." In what culture? Our answer is: culture in the sense of the Western tradition. Yet Western culture is only one among many cultures. By limiting ourselves to Western culture, do we not condemn liberal education to a kind of parochialism, and is not parochialism incompatible with the liberalism, the generosity, the openmindedness, of liberal education? Our notion of liberal education does not seem to fit an age which is aware of the fact that there is not *the* culture of *the* human mind but a variety of cultures. Obviously, "culture" if susceptible of being used in the plural is not quite the same thing as "culture" which is a *singulare tantum*, which can be used only in the singular. "Culture" is now no longer, as people say, an absolute but has become relative. It is not easy to say what culture susceptible of being used in the plural means. As a consequence of this obscurity people have suggested, explicitly or implicitly, that "culture" is any pattern of conduct common to any human group. Hence we do not hesitate to speak of the culture of suburbia or of the cultures of juvenile gangs both nondelinquent and delinquent. In other words, every human being outside of lunatic asylums is a cultured human being, for he participates in a culture. At the frontiers of research there arises the question as to whether there are not cultures also of inmates of lunatic asylums. If we contrast the present day usage of "culture" with the original meaning, it is as if someone would say that the cultivation of a garden may consist of the garden being littered with empty tin cans and whiskey bottles and used papers of various descriptions thrown around the garden at random. Having arrived at this point, we realize that we have lost our way somehow. Let us then make a fresh start by raising the question: what can liberal education mean here and now?

Liberal education is literate education of a certain kind: some sort of education in letters or through letters. There is no need to make a case for literacy; every voter knows that modern democracy stands or falls by literacy. In order to understand this need we must reflect on modern democracy. What is modern democracy? It was once said that democracy is the regime that stands or falls by virtue: a democracy is a regime in which all or most adults are men of virtue, and since virtue seems to require wisdom, a regime in which all or most adults are virtuous and wise, or the society in which all or most adults have developed their reason to a high degree, or *the* rational society. Democracy in a word is meant to be an aristocracy which has broadened into a universal aristocracy. Prior to the emergence of modern democracy some doubts were felt whether democracy thus understood is possible. As one of the two greatest minds among the theorists of democracy put it, "If there were a people consisting of gods, it would rule itself democratically. A government of such perfection is not suitable for human beings." This still and small voice has by now become a high-powered loudspeaker. There exists a whole science—the science which I among thousands profess to teach, political science—which so to speak has no other theme than the contrast between the original conception of democracy, or what one may call the ideal of democracy, and democracy as it is. According to an extreme view which is the predominant view in the profession, the ideal of democracy was a sheer delusion and the only thing which matters is the behavior of democracies and the behavior of men in democracies. Modern democracy, so far from being universal aristocracy, would be mass rule were it not for the fact that the mass cannot rule but is ruled by elites, i.e., groupings of men who for whatever reason are on top or have a fair chance to arrive at the top; one of the most important virtues required for the smooth working of democracy, as far as the mass is concerned, is said to be electoral apathy, i.e., lack of public spirit; not indeed the salt of the earth but the salt of modern democracy are those citizens who read nothing except the sports page and the comic section. Democracy is then not indeed mass rule but mass culture. A mass culture is a culture which can be appropriated by the meanest capacities without any intellectual and moral effort whatsoever and at a very low monetary price. But even a mass culture and precisely a mass culture requires a constant supply of what are called new ideas, which are the products of what are called creative minds: even singing commercials lose their appeal if they are not varied from time to time. But democracy, even if it is only regarded as the hard shell which protects the soft mass culture, requires in the long run qualities of an entirely different kind: qualities of dedication, of concentration, of breadth and of depth. Thus we understand most easily what liberal education means here and now. Liberal education is the counterpoison to mass culture, to the corroding effects of mass culture, to its inherent tendency to produce nothing but "specialists without spirit or vision and voluptuaries without heart." Liberal education is the ladder by which we try to ascend from mass democracy to democracy as originally meant. Liberal education is the necessary endeavor to found an aristocracy within democratic mass society. Liberal education reminds those members of a mass democracy who have ears to hear, of human greatness.

Someone might say that this notion of liberal education is merely political, that it dogmatically assumes the goodness of modern democracy. Can we not turn our backs on modern society? Can we not return to nature, to the life of preliterate tribes? Are we not crushed, nauseated, degraded by the mass of printed material, the graveyards of so many beautiful and majestic forests? It is not sufficient to say that this is mere romanticism, that we today cannot return to nature: may not

coming generations, after a man-wrought cataclysm, be compelled to live in illiterate tribes? Will our thoughts concerning thermonuclear wars not be affected by such prospects?
Certain it is that the horrors of mass culture (which include
guided tours to integer nature) render intelligible the longing
for a return to nature. An illiterate society at its best is a society ruled by age-old ancestral custom which it traces to original founders, gods or sons of gods or pupils of gods; since
there are no letters in such a society, the late heirs cannot be
in direct contact with the original founders; they cannot know
whether the fathers or grandfathers have not deviated from
what the original founders meant, or have not defaced the
divine message by merely human additions or subtractions; hence
an illiterate society cannot consistently act on its principle that
the best is the oldest. Only letters which have come down from
the founders can make it possible for the founders to speak
directly to the latest heirs. It is then self-contradictory to wish
to return to illiteracy. We are compelled to live with books.
But life is too short to live with any but the greatest books.
In this respect as well as in some others, we do well to take as
our model that one among the greatest minds who because of
his common sense is *the* mediator between us and the greatest
minds. Socrates never wrote a book but he read books. Let me
quote a statement of Socrates which says almost everything
that has to be said on our subject, with the noble simplicity
and quiet greatness of the ancients. "Just as others are pleased by a
good horse or dog or bird, I myself am pleased to an even higher
degree by good friends. . . . And the treasures of the wise men
of old which they left behind by writing them in books, I unfold
and go through them together with my friends, and if we see
something good, we pick it out and regard it as a great aim if
we thus become useful to one another." The man who reports this
utterance, adds the remark: "When I heard this, it seemed to
me both that Socrates was blessed and that he was leading those
listening to him toward perfect gentlemanship." This report is
defective since it does not tell us anything as to what Socrates
did regarding those passages in the books of the wise men of old
of which he did not know whether they were good. From an-

other report we learn that Euripides once gave Socrates the writing of Heraclitus and then asked him for his opinion about that writing. Socrates said: "What I have understood is great and noble; I believe this is also true of what I have not understood; but one surely needs for understanding that writing some special sort of a diver."

Education to perfect gentlemanship, to human excellence, liberal education consists in reminding oneself of human excellence, of human greatness. In what way, by what means does liberal education remind us of human greatness? We cannot think highly enough of what liberal education is meant to be. We have heard Plato's suggestion that education in the highest sense is philosophy. Philosophy is quest for wisdom or quest for knowledge regarding the most important, the highest, or the most comprehensive things; such knowledge, he suggested, is virtue and is happiness. But wisdom is inaccessible to man and hence virtue and happiness will always be imperfect. In spite of this, the philosopher, who, as such, is not simply wise, is declared to be the only true king; he is declared to possess all the excellences of which man's mind is capable, to the highest degree. From this we must draw the conclusion that we cannot be philosophers—that we cannot acquire the highest form of education. We must not be deceived by the fact that we meet many people who say that they are philosophers. For those people employ a loose expression which is perhaps necessitated by administrative convenience. Often they mean merely that they are members of philosophy departments. And it is as absurd to expect members of philosophy departments to be philosophers as it is to expect members of art departments to be artists. We cannot be philosophers but we can love philosophy; we can try to philosophize. This philosophizing consists at any rate primarily and in a way chiefly in listening to the conversation between the great philosophers or, more generally and more cautiously, between the greatest minds, and therefore in studying the great books. The greatest minds to whom we ought to listen are by no means exclusively the greatest minds of the West. It is merely an unfortunate necessity which prevents us from listening to the

greatest minds of India and of China: we do not understand
their languages, and we cannot learn all languages. To repeat,
liberal education consists in listening to the conversation among
the greatest minds. But here we are confronted with the overwhelming difficulty that this conversation does not take place
without our help—that in fact we must bring about that conversation. The greatest minds utter monologues. We must transform their monologues into a dialogue, their "side by side" into
a "together." The greatest minds utter monologues even when
they write dialogues. When we look at the Platonic dialogues, we
observe that there is never a dialogue among minds of the highest
order: all Platonic dialogues are dialogues between a superior
man and men inferior to him. Plato apparently felt that one
could not write a dialogue between two men of the highest order.
We must then do something which the greatest minds were
unable to do. Let us face this difficulty—a difficulty so great that
it seems to condemn liberal education as an absurdity. Since the
greatest minds contradict one another regarding the most important matters, they compel us to judge of their monologues;
we cannot take on trust what any one of them says. On the
other hand we cannot but notice that we are not competent
to be judges. This state of things is concealed from us by a
number of facile delusions. We somehow believe that our point
of view is superior, higher than those of the greatest minds—
either because our point of view is that of our time, and our
time, being later than the time of the greatest minds, can be
presumed to be superior to their times; or else because we
believe that each of the greatest minds was right from his point
of view but not, as he claims, simply right: we know that there
cannot be *the* simply true substantive view but only a simply
true formal view; that formal view consists in the insight that
every comprehensive view is relative to a specific perspective,
or that all comprehensive views are mutually exclusive and none
can be simply true. The facile delusions which conceal from us
our true situation all amount to this, that we are, or can be,
wiser than the wisest men of the past. We are thus induced
to play the part not of attentive and docile listeners, but of

impresarios or lion-tamers. Yet we must face our awesome situation, created by the necessity that we try to be more than attentive and docile listeners, namely, judges, and yet we are not competent to be judges. As it seems to me, the cause of this situation is that we have lost all simply authoritative traditions in which we could trust, the *nomos* which gave us authoritative guidance, because our immediate teachers and teachers' teachers believed in the possibility of a simply rational society. Each of us here is compelled to find his bearings by his own powers however defective they may be.

We have no comfort other than that inherent in this activity. Philosophy, we have learned, must be on its guard against the wish to be edifying—philosophy can only be intrinsically edifying. We cannot exert our understanding without from time to time understanding something of importance; and this act of understanding may be accompanied by the awareness of our understanding, by the understanding of understanding, by *noesis noeseos*, and this is so high, so pure, so noble an experience that Aristotle could ascribe it to his God. This experience is entirely independent of whether what we understand primarily is pleasing or displeasing, fair or ugly. It leads us to realize that all evils are in a sense necessary if there is to be understanding. It enables us to accept all evils which befall us and which may well break our hearts in the spirit of good citizens of the city of God. By becoming aware of the dignity of the mind, we realize the true ground of the dignity of man and therewith the goodness of the world, whether we understand it as created or as uncreated, which is the home of man because it is the home of the human mind.

Liberal education, which consists in the constant intercourse with the greatest minds, is a training in the highest form of modesty, not to say of humility. It is at the same time a training in boldness: it demands from us the complete break with the noise, the rush, the thoughtlessness, the cheapness of the Vanity Fair of the intellectuals as well as of their enemies. It demands from us the boldness implied in the resolve to regard the accepted views as mere opinions, or to regard the average opinions as extreme opinions which are at least as likely to be wrong as the most strange or the least popular opinions. Liberal education is liberation from vulgarity. The Greeks had a beautiful word for "vulgarity"; they called it *apeirokalia*, lack of experience in things beautiful. Liberal education supplies us with experience in things beautiful.

A REDEFINITION OF
EDUCATION / *MARGARET MEAD*

WHEN WE look realistically at today's world and become aware of what the actual problems of learning are, our conception of education changes radically. Although the educational system remains basically unchanged, we are no longer dealing primarily with the *vertical* transmission of the tried and true by the old, mature, and experienced teacher to the young, immature, and inexperienced pupil in the classroom.

This was the system of education developed in a stable, slowly changing culture. By itself, vertical transmission of knowledge no longer adequately serves the purposes of education in a world of rapid change.

What is needed and what we are already moving toward is the inclusion of another whole dimension of learning: the *lateral* transmission, to every sentient member of society, of what has just been discovered, invented, created, manufactured, or marketed.

This need for lateral transmission exists no less in the classroom and laboratory than it does on the assembly line with its working force of experienced and raw workmen. The man who teaches another individual the new mathematics or the use of a newly invented tool is not sharing knowledge he acquired years ago. He learned what was new yesterday, and his pupil must learn it today.

The whole teaching-and-learning continuum, once tied in an orderly and productive way to the passing of generations and the growth of the child into a man, has exploded in our faces. Yet even as we try to catch hold of and patch up the pieces, we fail to recognize what has happened.

We have moved into a period in which the break with the past provides an opportunity for creating a new framework for activity in almost every field—but in each field the fact that there has been a break must be rediscovered. In education there has been up to now no real recognition of the extent to which our present system is outmoded.

Historians point sagely to the last two educational crises—the first of which ended with the establishment of the universal elementary school and the second with the establishment of the universal high school—and with remarkable logic and lack of imagination they predict that the present crisis will follow the same pattern.

According to such predictions, the crisis will last until 1970, when it will end with the establishment of universal college education, accessible in principle to all young Americans.

Implicit in this prediction is a series of other dubious assumptions, such as these:

Our educational system has fallen behind in something and should therefore arrange to catch up; our difficulties are due to the "bulge," the host of babies that tricked the statisticians; the pendulum is swinging back to sense—to discipline and dunce caps, switches and multiplication tables.

But in the midst of the incessant discussion and the search for scapegoats to take the blame for what everyone admits is a parlous state, extraordinarily little attention is being paid to basic issues. Everyone simply wants more of what we already have: more children in more schools for more hours studying more of something.

Likewise, scant attention is paid to the fact that two great new educational agencies, the armed services and industry, have entered the field, and there is little awareness of the ways in which operations in these institutions are altering traditional education.

But most important, the pattern itself is hardly questioned, for we *think* we know what education is and what a good education ought to be. However deficient we may be as a people, as taxpayers, or as educators, we may be actualizing our ideals.

An occasional iconoclast can ask: "Wouldn't it be fine if we could scrap our whole school system and start anew?" But he gets no hearing because everyone knows that what he is saying is nonsense. Wishful dreams of starting anew are obviously impractical, but this does not mean that someone should not ask these crucial questions:

Is our present historic idea of education suitable for people in the mid-twentieth century, who have a life expectancy of 70 years, and who live in a world of automation and global communication, ready to begin space exploration and aware of the possibility of bringing about the suicide of the entire human species?

Is it not possible that the problem of the educational system's obsolescence goes beyond such issues as methods of teaching reading or physics, or the most desirable age for leaving school, or the payment of teachers, or the length of summer holidays, or the number of years best devoted to college?

Is not the break between past and present—and so the whole problem of outdating in our educational system—related to a change in the rate of change? For change has become so rapid that adjustment cannot be left to the next generation. Adults must —not once, but continually—take in, adjust to, use, and make innovations in a steady stream of discovery and new conditions.

Is it not possible that an educational system that was designed to teach what was known to little children and to a selected few young men may not fit a world in which the most important factors in everyone's life are those things that are not yet, but soon will be, known?

Is it not equally possible that our present definition of a pupil or a student is out of date when we define the learner as a child (or at best an immature person) who is entitled to moral protection and subsistence in a dependency position and who is denied the moral autonomy that is accorded to an adult?

Looking at our educational system today, we can see that in various ways it combines these different functions: the protection of the child against exploitation and the protection of society against precocity and inexperience; the maintenance of learners in a state of moral and economic dependency; giving to all children the special, wider education once reserved for those of privileged groups, in an attempt to form the citizen of a democracy as once the son of a noble house was formed; the teaching of complex and specialized skills which, under our complex system of division of labor, is too difficult and time-consuming for each set of parents to master or to hand on to their own children; the transmission of something which the parents' generation does *not* know (in the case of immigrants with varied cultural and linguistic backgrounds) to children whom the authorities or the parents wish to have educated.

To these multiple functions of an educational system, which, in a slowly changing society, were variously performed, we have added slowly and reluctantly a quite new function: *education for rapid and self-conscious adaptation to a changing world.*

That we have as yet failed to recognize the new character of change is apparent in a thousand ways. Despite the fact that a subject taught to college freshmen may have altered basically by the time the same students are seniors, it is still said that colleges are able to give students "a good education"—finished, wrapped, sealed with a degree.

Upon getting a bachelor's degree, a student can decide to "go on" to a higher degree because he has not as yet "completed" his education, that is, the lump of the known which he has decided to bite off. But a student who has once let a year go by after he is "out of school" does not "go *on*," but rather "goes *back*" to school.

And as we treat education as the right of a minor who has not yet completed high school, just so we equate marriage and parenthood with getting a diploma; both indicate that one's education is "finished."

Consistent with our conception of what a student is, our educational institutions are places where we keep "children" for a shorter or longer period. The length of time depends in part on their intelligence and motivation and in part on their parents' incomes and the immediately recognized national needs for particular skills or types of training.

Once they have left, we regard them as in some sense finished, neither capable of nor in need of further "education," for we still believe that education should come all in one piece, or rather, in a series of connected pieces, each presented as a whole at the elementary, secondary, and the college level. All other behaviors are aberrant.

So we speak of "interrupted" education—that is, education which has been broken into by sickness, delinquency, or military service—and we attempt to find means of repairing this interruption. Indeed, the whole GI bill, which in a magnificent way gave millions of young men a chance for a different kind of education than they would otherwise have got, was conceived of primarily as a means of compensating young men for an unsought but unavoidable interruption.

Thus we avoid facing the most vivid truth of the new age: *No one will live all his life in the world into which he was born, and no one will die in the world in which he worked in his maturity.*

For those who work on the growing edge of science, technology, or the arts, contemporary life changes at even shorter intervals. Often, only a few months may elapse before something which previously was easily taken for granted must be unlearned or transformed to fit the new state of knowledge or practice.

In today's world, no one can "complete an education." The students we need are not just children who are learning to read and write, plus older students, conceived of as minors, who are either "going on" with or "going back" to specialized education. Rather, we need children *and* adolescents *and* young *and* mature *and* "senior" adults, each of whom is learning at the appropriate pace and with all the special advantages and disadvantages of experience peculiar to his own age.

Each and every one of these is a learner, not only of the old and tried—the alphabet or multiplication tables or Latin declensions or French irregular verbs or the binomial theorem—but of new, hardly tried theories and methods: pattern analysis, general system theory, space lattices, cybernetics, and so on.

Learning of this kind must go on, not only at special times and in special places, but all through production and consumption—from the technician who must handle a new machine to the factory supervisor who must introduce its use, the union representative who must interpret it to the men, the foreman who must keep the men working, the salesman who must service a new device or find markets for it, the housewife who must understand how to care for a new material, the mother who must answer the questions of a four-year-old child.

In this world, the age of the teacher is no longer necessarily relevant. For instance, children teach grandparents how to manage TV, young expediters come into the factory along with the new equipment, and young men invent automatic programing for computers over which their seniors struggle.

This, then, is what we call the *lateral transmission* of knowledge. It is not an outpouring of knowledge from the "wise old teacher" into the minds of young pupils, as in vertical transmission. Rather, it is a sharing of knowledge by the informed with the uninformed, whatever their ages. The primary prerequisite for the learner is the desire to know.

To facilitate this lateral transmission of knowledge, we need to redefine what we mean by primary and secondary education. We need to stop thinking that free and, when necessary, subsidized education is appropriate *only* when it is preliminary to an individual's work experience.

Instead of adding more and more years of compulsory education (which would further confuse the meaning of education and the purpose of schools), we need to separate primary and secondary education in an entirely new way:

By *primary education* we would mean the stage of education in which all children are taught what they need to know in order to be fully human in the world in which they are growing up— including the basic skills of reading and writing and a basic knowledge of numbers, money, geography, transportation and communication, the law, and the nations of the world.

By *secondary education* we would mean an education that is based on primary education, and that can be obtained *in any amount* and *at any period* during the individual's whole lifetime.

After agreeing upon this redefinition, we could begin to deal effectively with the vast new demands that are being made on us. The high schools would be relieved of the nonlearners. (It would be essential, of course, that industry, government, or some other social group accept the responsibility of employing or otherwise occupying these persons.)

But, more important, men and women, instead of preparing for a single career to which—for lack of any alternative—they must stick during their entire active lives, would realize that they might learn something else. Women, after their children became older, could be educated for particular new tasks, instead of facing the rejection that today is related to fear about the difficulty of acquiring new learning in middle age.

Whatever their age, those obtaining a secondary education at any level (high school, college, or beyond) would be in school because they *wanted* to learn and *wanted* to be there *at that time*.

In an educational system of this kind, we could give primary education and protection to children as well as protection and sensitive supervision to adolescents. We could back up to the hilt the potentiality of every human being—of whatever age—to learn at any level.

The right to obtain secondary education when and where the individual could use it would include not only the right of access to existing conventional types of schools but also the right of access to types of work training not yet or only now being developed—new kinds of apprenticeship and also new kinds of work teams.

In thinking about an effective educational system, we should recognize that the adolescent's need and right to work is as great as (perhaps greater than) his immediate need and right to study. And we must recognize that the adult's need and right to study more is as great as (perhaps greater than) his need and right to hold the same job until he is 65.

We cannot accomplish the essential educational task merely by keeping children and young adults—whom we treat like children—in school longer. We can do it by creating an educational system in which all individuals will be assured of the secondary and higher education they want and can use any time throughout their entire lives.

WHAT KIND OF AMERICAN CIVILIZATION DO WE WANT? / F. S. C. NORTHROP

IN 1950 the Cultural Division of the South East Asia Treaty Organization called a conference at Bangkok. Its concern was modern technology in Asian societies. Two facts were reported which make one ask whether we have the kind of civilization we want.

Mr. Tom Harrisson, representing Sarawak, reported that a more culturally isolated people than his neighbors on the island of Borneo do not exist. Little reaches them except a few radios and three broadcasts from Indonesia, Australia, and Communist China. Since they know none of the languages spoken, what they hear from abroad is not understood. Nevertheless, these broadcasts have disrupted their folk dances of high quality. By capturing their ears and imaginations, the mere beat of boogie-woogie has corrupted their aesthetic standards and is destroying their customs.

Ambassador W. R. Crocker, representing Australia, called attention to the English reading material from the Free World available on street-corner stands in Bangkok. He testified that it is similar to what he found at Jakarta when he was Ambassador to Indonesia. He suggested that it is all too similar also to what exists in Australia, Canada, the United States, and even Great Britain. Needless to say, it portrays younger people of the most vulgar aesthetic taste with apparently no moral scruples whatever whose main concern is with sex at its crudest, making money by any means, and whipping out a revolver upon the slightest of whims. Many mollifying factors though there be, this is the image of the

Free World which the marriage of mass communication with the businessman's laissez-faire profit motive is creating today both abroad and at home. It appears, Ambassador Crocker concluded, that there is a Gresham's law of culture as well as of money at work by which everywhere the bad is driving out the good.

To appreciate the full effect abroad of this image, the classical Asian, medieval European, and Latin American conception of proper relations between the sexes in public must be understood. In Confucian China, as in many Mexican villages today, a husband and wife do not walk down the street side by side. It is immoral also for even an engaged couple to meet unless the parents of both are continuously present. Imagine the impact upon the people when they see American movies, to say nothing about the "personal confessions" in the paperbacks. In 1950 the British educated editor of India's excellent magazine of art, *Marg*, said to the writer: "If you think some of your American movies are vulgar, you should see some which are created by young Indians who are copying yours and who know nothing of the artistic and other cultural standards and achievements of the West. Having been thus led by the influence of your movies to repudiate the aesthetic standards and social customs of their own great civilization and knowing next to nothing of yours, they have no standards whatever to guide them. The result often is that compared with some Indian movies, the most vulgar of yours are models of aesthetic refinement and sensitivity." The only moral and artistic standards they know being thus flouted, the conclusion follows easily that the Americans have no aesthetic or social good taste whatever and that for them "anything goes" providing one makes money in the process.

The ill effects are political as well as cultural. Once this image of America arises, it becomes natural for Mr. Arnold Toynbee to reply to an American secretary of state's broadcast about "massive retaliation at a time and place of one's own choosing" with "No annihilation without representation!" and for Asian statesmen to conclude also that the Americans, like the youth in their movies and paperbacks, are "trigger-happy" with the atomic bomb and hence not to be trusted as allies in protecting the Free World.

This is the trouble with neglecting the cultural factor in international politics. Because a secretary of state neglected the advice of cultural officers and other career diplomats in his own Department who are experienced in sensing the diverse cultural and political mentalities of the nations to which they are assigned and are expert in reporting objectively on the most likely foreign response to anything America does, the late Mr. Dulles defeated his own purposes. Instead of winning—through experienced diplomatic negotiations, tailor-made to the unique cultural and political concerns of each European, Latin American, African, Middle Eastern and Asian nation—the assent of his allies to his "new" foreign policy before he announced it, thereby giving political and cultural leaders abroad the time to prepare the minds of their own people for what he "really meant" by "massive retaliation . . . at one's own choosing," he unwittingly and quite unnecessarily drove into positive anti-Americanism even people like Mr. Toynbee, Pandit Nehru, and hundreds of millions of Europeans and Asians behind them, who want to believe the best about the United States. With far less money given to the Cultural Division and career diplomats than it costs to replace with American soldiers and weapons the military support thus lost, such unfortunate political and military consequences of the neglect of the cultural image of ourselves which we create abroad, could have been avoided.

Nor were Secretary Dulles' opposite numbers in the previous Democratic administrations entirely different. The major foreign policy adviser and Chairman of the Planning Board of Secretary Acheson's State Department was Mr. George F. Kennan. Quite contrary to his practice in understanding the Soviet Union, Mr. Kennan in his foreign policy theorizing tells us that "the moral-legal state of mind," that is, the cultural approach, is quite misplaced in international relations and that "power-balancing" "should" be used instead. This is equally self-defeating as the neutralism which it generated in South Asia following the Korean United Nations police action shows since it made the Soviet Russians' Mr. Malik's point for him when he returned to the Security Council. This point was that the presence of American forces in Korea was not the United Nations morally and legally authorized police action that it purported to be but was instead a militaristic power move upon the part of the United States to get its troops on Asian soil, into which America had duped her Asian and European allies.

Republican Candidate Eisenhower fell into the same Hobbesian error as Mr. Kennan when, in an irresponsible appeal for votes in his first election campaign, the General insisted against President Truman that the American boys in Korea were "in a war" and not in a United Nations legally authorized police action.

This power-politics philosophy of American foreign policy of the Republican candidate of 1951 and the Kennan-minded Democrats inevitably had the effect of reinforcing the image of America abroad as a military- and power-minded people rather than a morally and legally principled nation. It also left America morally and legally impotent when the Soviet tanks crushed Hungary. It is probably because of the danger of such a broken American image of herself that our Founding Fathers warned us explicitly against following the Machiavellian and Hobbesian power politics of eighteenth- and nineteenth-century Europe in our foreign policy. Jefferson—to whom our Founding Fathers entrusted the major share of the writing of their first foreign policy document, the Declaration of Independence—had studied the legal and political philosophy of the ancient Greeks, the Stoic Roman lawyers, and all the moderns including Hobbes, Locke, Hume, and Rousseau. Jefferson's letters make it unequivocally clear that in the type of legal and political system which they created and in their foreign policy, the Founding Fathers' choice was between the political philosophies of Hobbes and Locke—and that they followed Locke. This is the point of Jefferson's statement that in his opinion "the three greatest men the world had ever produced [were] Bacon, Newton, and Locke." This, rather than isolationism, is the point also of the warning issued to us by Washington, Jefferson, and Hamilton against "entangling alliances" with "the imperialistic nations of [eighteenth- and nineteenth-century] Europe."

Unfortunately this counsel has not been followed. The result is that due to a Kennan-minded Hobbesian Democratic foreign policy and an Eisenhower-minded Republican foreign policy which has oscillated between a Hobbesian intepretation of what happened in Korea and an international legal interpretation of

British, French, and Israeli behavior at Suez, American international leadership in both parties has made America present a broken image of herself abroad. This is doubly tragic since it has occurred at the very time when the majority of Continental Europeans, as Continental European Union shows, and the majority of Britishers, as the existence of the British Commonwealth demonstrates, have repudiated Hobbes for Locke.

The domestic consequences are equally reactionary and serious. Only yesterday we read about the absurdity which occurs when three present Democratic foreign policy makers—Messrs. Acheson, Nitze, and King—whose expertness is that of the black-letter positive lawyer, wrote "a major foreign policy document" on military weapons, the efficiency of which they are obviously incompetent to judge. Also this Democratic foreign policy makes the professional soldiers who select their own successors the only competent deciders of foreign policy. Thus, again, military men and instruments are given primary roles in the image of America which American civilians are creating, thereby continuing the defeat of her purposes. Also, military men whose expertness is in instrumental values are forced, often against their own best judgment and wishes, to divert their attention from their own more-than-full-time job, to decide cultural and political goal-value questions in which they have no experience and little first-hand competence. Thus civilians in the State Department would behave like amateurish third-rate soldiers, and soldiers in the White House, Pentagon, and war colleges are forced to behave like amateurish second-rate politicians. The unfortunate de facto result—as seen objectively from abroad and as Sputnik has made evident within— is an America which in the realm of military instrumental values is dangerously close to being second rate and in the even more important domain of goal values is presenting a politically confused or crude and an aesthetically vulgar image of herself to the world. This image was not improved by Vice President Nixon's public exchange with Premier Khrushchev in Moscow, as the British reaction reported in the *New York Times* of July 26, 1959, clearly demonstrates.

But some will say: "Washington, Jefferson, and Hamilton did not have the Communist divisions and hydrogen bombs to face.

Conditions are different today. Security must come first."

Let us reflect on what this means. It means what it says, which is that physical power and physical security are more important than civilized human beings who are the sole reason for physical power and security. In short, it means a self-contradictory and a persistingly self-defeating America.

Also, instead of curbing and eventually civilizing the Communists, it insures that we do precisely what Stalin designed the cold war to do—namely, cause us to abdicate the Lockean foreign policy ideals of the Declaration of Independence and the domestic religious and civil liberties of our Lockean Bill of Rights, thereby enabling the Communists to be feted at Bandung as the sole defenders throughout Africa, the Middle East, and Asia of the ideals for which the America of 1776 and 1791 stands. In short, the result is to hand the entire idealistic religious, legal, and political goal-value battle for the imaginations and loyalties of the youth of the world over to the Communists with little if any competition from us at the ideological-cultural level.

We must not fool ourselves. The Communists do not present themselves to Africans and Asians in terms of pressure for military bases or for the receipt of economic handouts. They present themselves instead in terms of their goal-value philosophy of an ideal world. In 1950 on the street-corner stands of Bombay, for example, one could buy for a few pennies the technical philosophical classics of Marx, Engels, and Lenin which define this ideal. On his return from India in 1950, the writer was told by informed people in Cairo that young Egyptian Communists were studying the Islamic classics in the world's leading Islamic university, thereby identifying themselves with the best in that great civilization, while also teaching their fellow Egyptian students the technical philosophical doctrines and ideals of the Communists. Consequently, the image which Stalin's Russia and Mao's China were then giving to the youth of Asia, Islam, and Africa was not that of youthful social parasites obsessed with sex, money-making, and gun play, but of a serious and poor Russian and Chinese youth, like themselves, who were working long hours in the classroom, the laboratory, and the factory to master the Marxist philosophy, the mathematics, medicine, and technology necessary to implement and protect the achievement of a specific philosophically defined goal-value ideal for all their people.

One looked in vain in 1950 in the street-corner stands of New Delhi, Karachi, or Cairo for the goal-value classics of America and the Free World. Instead, the literature discribed later by Ambassador Crocker at Bangkok was in its place.

It is to be noted that Australia's political scientist and diplomat did not put the blame for the present operation of a Gresham's law of culture solely on modern technology and the emphasis upon quantity at the expense of quality which it makes possible. Ambassador Crocker noted that the veneration of the businessman's profit motive as the highest good is also responsible. Certainly it comes near to being in major part culpable because technological instruments are normatively neutral with respect to what they communicate. It appears, therefore, that the vulgar image of themselves which the peoples of the Free World are exporting has its source in the false inversion of instrumental and goal values in which they have indulged at home.

Is this the America we want? If not, then must we not ask ourselves the following more specific questions?

Does creative art and the cultivation of aesthetic sensitivity to the artistic standards of our own and other great civilizations enjoy the place of primacy in our educational system and in the civilizing of our movie producers, commercial publishers, television viewers, and book buyers which an America of quality requires? Is the Cultural Division of the State Department listened to with sufficient seriousness when Congress examines the budget, or by our secretaries of state when they make major policy decisions and announcements? Do we possess a Cultural Division and Planning Board in the State Department composed of experienced diplomats, cultural anthropologists, and experts in the world's various cultural and political philosophies, including our own, who are capable of framing a consistent and principled foreign policy that is (1) based on the fact that our Founding Fathers created an America in which both domestic legal and foreign policy is grounded in the religious and political philosophy of Locke and Jefferson and the later Lincoln rather than in the philosophy of Machiavelli and Hobbes; and (2) capable of winning the joyful support of men like Mr. Toynbee, Pandit Nehru, Premier Nkrumah, and hundreds of millions of Europeans, Middle Easterners, Asians, and Africans who are now making their own Lockean and Jeffersonian declarations of independence?

Finally, are men whose expertness is in the instrumental values of the soldier, the businessman, or the latter's corporation lawyer, or whose foreign policy philosophy is that of instrumental material power, likely to express in their specific practical political deeds the primacy of concern with goal-value cultural and philosophical ideals which is required if one is to be an effective diplomat or a nonself-defeating secretary of state? In short, has not the time come in both political parties to create a single, truly American foreign policy by putting it in the care of fresh and more philosophically specific and imaginative minds who believe that the Lockean philosophy of goal values of our Founding Fathers still has something to say for itself in both domestic law and foreign policy?

If the answer to the foregoing questions be yes, certain additional questions follow immediately. Must not religious and political philosophy be given a place of primacy beside the cultivation of aesthetic sensitivity in the general education of everyone? More specifically, must not the religious philosophy of toleration and the separation of church and state of John Locke's *Letter Concerning Toleration* by required reading for every student? As the English social historian, Trevelyan, tells us, many people previously advocated toleration for reasons of religious or political expediency when they were in the minority or wanted freedom from religious wars, but it was with Locke for the first time that toleration became regarded as a positive good in and for itself even when one was in the majority. Must not also the legal and political philosophy of the Stoic Roman lawyers and Cicero, of Locke's *Lectures Concerning Natural Law* and *Of Civil Government*, together with the letters of Jefferson and the *Federalist Papers*, be given a place of primacy in the general educational system, the war colleges, and the training of foreign service officers? Is there any reason also why these philosophical classics should not be made available in penny editions, translated into every native language and dialect for all the world to read?

Might it not be well also to acquaint everyone in the United States with Hobbes' *Leviathan*, the nineteenth-century English jurist Austin's *Province of Jurisprudence Determined*, Judge Learned Hand's *The Spirit of Liberty*, and essays on *The Bill of Rights* which derive, by way of Thayer of the 1890 Harvard Law School and Austin, from Hobbes? Then everyone will know the difference between the type of legal and political system of "checks and balances" based on Locke which our Founding Fathers created and the type of democratic positive legal institutions based on Hobbes which the British created and into which Mr. Justice Frankfurter sometimes, and Judge Learned Hand always, would now have us transform the institutions created by our Founding Fathers. Were this done, there would certainly not now be the confusion concerning whether it is the Chief Justice Warren and Justices Black, Brennan, and Douglas wing of the Supreme Court or the Justice Frankfurter-focused wing which represents the original conception of the Constitution and its Bill of Rights.

The heart of the difference between Locke and Hobbes is this. The former does not trust the locating of the entire political sovereignty of even a democratic government in any one branch of government. Consequently it divides political sovereignty between the three branches. It has a directly elected president who stays in office until the end of his term even when his party loses majority control of the legislative branch and who also has the power, which every American president has exercised, of vetoing majority approved legislative statutes for any reason he may choose to give. Similarly, in order to give legal protection to the religious and political beliefs of dissenters and to locate part of the political sovereignty in the judicial branch, the Lockean philosophy of democratic government as applied by Jefferson, Madison, the Adamses, and our other Founding Fathers adds a Bill of Rights which the federal judges are legally bound to interpret as law and use as a standard, not as Judge Hand would have us believe to "introduce a third legislature," but to measure the substantive content of the legislature's statutes in the legal protection of religious and civil liberties.

The first draft of the federal Constitution was sent by both

Washington and Madison to Jefferson who was then Ambassador to France. Jefferson immediately replied that this constitution would not do, since it did not contain a "declaration of rights." Madison in his reply to Jefferson agreed, while adding certain reasons put forward to the contrary. On March 15, 1789, Jefferson replied to Madison as follows: "In the arguments in favor of a declaration of rights . . . one which has great weight with me [is] the legal check which it puts into the hands of the judiciary."

The word "legal" in the foregoing quotation from Jefferson speaks for itself. It means that the Founding Fathers who were persuaded in part by Jefferson's arguments to add the Bill of Rights to the federal Constitution intended it to be interpreted as law by the federal courts. They did not construe it to mean what Judge Hand, following Thayer, Austin, and Hobbes, would now have it mean, namely, mere "admonitions to forbearance" or "counsels of moderation" which, if the legislators choose to ignore, a federal "judge of principle" will do nothing to redress. Making it doubly clear that the Bill of Rights is to be interpreted as law, Jefferson added in his letter of March 15, 1789, that "the executive, in our [state and federal] governments, is not the sole, it is scarcely the principal object of my jealousy. The tyranny of the legislatures is the most formidable dread at present, and will be for many years."

In the Hobbesian theory of democracy on the other hand, which the positive portion of the British unwritten constitution follows (the living customs of Britain's unwritten constitution being Lockean), the whole of political sovereignty is placed in the legislative branch. Thus in Great Britain today, as in most of the other democracies of the contemporary world, the head of the executive branch of government is merely the leader of the majority party in the legislature, having no veto power over legislation approved by the majority and going out of office the moment his party loses majority control of the legislature. Similarly, no British court can declare a statute approved by the majority of the House of Commons to be illegal. The legal philosophy of Hobbes, Austin, Thayer, and Judge Learned Hand fits the positive law of Great Britain's unwritten constitution, but does not fit the legal and political system of the United States. The practical effect, therefore, of accepting the legal philosophy of Judge Learned Hand and the Justice Frankfurter wing of the present Supreme Court will be to transform the American legal and political system, which was based on Locke rather than Hobbes, into the Hobbesian positive legal portion of the British system.

Again two more questions arise: Is the latter the kind of America we want? In other words, do we want to follow Hobbes in our domestic as well as foreign politics? Or do we want to win back the confidence of the majority of Britishers who are now Lockeans, the majority of Continental Europeans who are now Stoic Roman internationalists, and the majority of the people of the world generally who are now issuing their own Lockean and Jeffersonian declarations of independence, by returning to both the domestic legal and the foreign policy philosophy of our Founding Fathers?

Whatever our choice, one thing is clear. To be a civilized American without knowing the religious, moral, legal, and political philosophy which specifies what American civilization and the world's freedom as we understand it mean, is to attempt the impossible. Hence, the philosophy of our goal values must take its place as primary beside the cultivation of aesthetic sensitivity in our entire educational system.

But even this is not enough. Sputnik has shown that in addition to the seeking of beauty and justice there must also be the seeking of mathematical truth.

Admiral Rickover has told us something which every general and admiral knows who may find himself carrying on a legally authorized international police action with second-rate weapons. American youth who are self-indulgent or concerned mainly with extracurricular activities during their schooling will not do. What has to be realized is that the practical man by himself is today the most impractical fellow on earth. Without the pioneer leadership in the frontier of human knowledge of the most formally minded theorists in symbolic logic, pure mathematics, and theoretical as well as experimental physics, the practical man knows, if he is honest with himself, that he will be a failure. Devoid of the most mathematical and even the most philosophical theory of natural science which Einstein, Heisenberg and countless others, such as Willard Gibbs, Maxwell, Kant, Leibniz, Newton, Euclid, Eudoxus, and Democritus pursued in and for its own sake, the practical instruments of today's world would not be. Moreover, unless today's and tomorrow's youth pioneer beyond Gibbs, Einstein, and Heisenberg, the military and industrial instruments of tomorrow's so-called practical people are likely to be second rate. This is why one commits instrumental as well as moral suicide when one puts sensitivity to money-making in the market place ahead of the seeking and telling of truth for its own sake in theoretical natural science and its philosophy.

But the symbolic logic and the advanced mathematics that are required to keep ahead in one's military and industrial instruments and strategy cannot be learned on the spur of the moment when the defense of freedom may become urgently necessary. Nor can they be studied for a while and then dropped to be picked up a year or two later where one left them off. When the writer was on the Executive Committee of Yale College some twenty years ago, it became evident that able students of high standing in mathematics who, for sickness or any other reason, were forced to drop their studies for even a year, on returning to college frequently failed their next course in mathematics. The practical moral should be clear: training in formal thinking, including English grammar, symbolic logic, and mathematics, must be given a place of continuous primacy in the educational system beside the seeking of beauty and tolerant religious, moral, legal, and political philosophy. Only if these three things are done is it likely that America can keep her ideals in the forefront of what she is doing to win the confidence of free men everywhere and at the same time possess first-rate instruments for protecting and implementing these ideals.

It will be said that the addition of these subjects in the degree indicated to the present educational curriculum is impossible since it is already overcrowded. Such a judgment will not, however, stand careful analysis. The plain fact at present is that most of the subjects now taught in the curriculum are not understood. The reason is that most of them require one or more of the three basic disciplines noted above for their understanding. How, for example, can a student possibly understand anything if he is incapable, as is presently the case with many students entering college, of framing semantically clear and grammatical sentences for an attempted paper? How can a person possibly distinguish sensed fact from inferred theory in natural or social science if he does not have the aesthetic sensitivity to distinguish (1) the impressionistic sensuous images which the senses convey to him from (2) the directly unobservable, theoretically known, and mathematically defined scientific objects which he infers from these impressionistic aesthetic sensed images? How can a student, a teacher, or a statesman avoid being anything but confused about his normative religious, moral, legal, and political ideals and decisions if he is unaware of normative philosophy and the difference between a statement concerning what ought to be and a nonnormative statement about what is the case in fact? To put the three aforementioned basic subjects first in our educational system will be, therefore, to clarify the curriculum and to economize in the time it takes to civilize our citizens.

In any event, two things are clear: there is an American civilization of quality. We can have it if we want it.

EDUCATION IN ACTION:
ACTION THROUGH SOCIETY

HUMANISTS AND
GENERALISTS / *HENRY M. WRISTON*

I HAVE never heard of an analytical survey of the state of leadership that was likely to produce a complacent attitude. That statement can be applied to any field which is subjected to analysis.

Complaints about education and its deficiencies—due to lack of leadership—have been the standard pattern of discussion throughout the nineteenth and twentieth centuries in America. The pace of social change always appears both more rapid and more decisive than the adjustment, not to say leadership, in the educational process. One sardonic educator summed up his view with the remark that it took about fifty years for half the educators to accept a new idea, however good. I can find the same thought, differently expressed, over a century ago. There is no point, therefore, in looking to the past to find a Golden Age of American education.

With the American genius—or weakness—for voluntary organization, we have had more committees, councils, societies, and associations to promote education than all the rest of the world put together. Yet the sad fact emerges that the larger part of their energies has gone into restrictive practices. They have not looked to recruitment of leaders, or to the development of leadership, but toward excluding from the guild any who do not meet "standards." The criteria by which the standards are defined have little to do with substance, and far too much with form. By deliberate design competent people are excluded from teaching because they have not performed some ritual of training. It is hardly too much to say that the net effect of alleged standards has been to inhibit leadership rather than stimulate it. Salary policies, enforced by organizational pressure, have had a like negative effect. Protection of those in the trade, including those who should be eliminated, has been the normal practice. Defense of the weak rather than scope for the strong has been the goal.

Analyses of our government are almost uniformly negative. The deficiencies of the democratic process as such, and of our forms and methods of government specifically, have occupied the minds of men ever since the Declaration of Independence. Conspicuous among our shortcomings has been the want of political thinkers of a high order. The government of today is radically different from the government designed—or codified, if it does not seem to you very "original"—in 1787. Critics can assert upon good evidence that it has been shaped and modified by crisis and circumstance, by pressure and politics, rather than by reason and intellect. Proposals, however logical, evoke only mild interest, and virtually no response in action. There is an all but complete divorce between the thinkers and the practitioners of politics. To see how serious is this breach, it is necessary only to recall the terms of opprobrium heaped upon those who try to bridge the gap; "egghead" is only a recent example, the successor of a long line of earlier epithets.

The history of analyses is even more pessimistic when one turns to the arts. They are poorly supported. Symphony orchestras and deficits are so closely associated in the public mind as to seem virtually synonymous. Opera has been dependent primarily upon Europe to supply singers for its leading roles. The number of opera companies which has survived in America is far too small. There is inadequate opportunity for training, and even less for the acquisition of experience. Europe is the Mecca for both.

Painting, sculpture, architecture are in similar case. Their economic foundations are shaky, facilities for education are inadequate in quantity and quality, and opportunities for expression far too few. These things remain true, despite the fact that the public interest has grown astoundingly. Attendance at exhibits—once a problem—runs to vast figures. It is far greater than the over-advertised attendance at sports events. Yet, under these circumstances, our greatest public museum is forced to curtail its schedule and close one day a week for lack of funds.

The customary explanation for most of these deficiencies is historical. In a new country energy was absorbed in taming the land, in the westward trek, in building a standard of living which is the wonder of the world. It is in the economic field that names of leaders spring to mind: Rockefeller, Carnegie, Ford, on the one side; Green, Hillman, Lewis on the other. Such names are mere symbols; there has been a succession of giants in production, finance, marketing, and a striking number of labor managers whose leadership has been conspicuous, not only in America but in the labor movement around the world. It is a notable fact that when any such list is examined, it will be observed that nearly all the outstanding leaders were self-taught. They came up through the ranks, not by grace of wealth, or status, or privilege, but by energy, shrewdness, persistence, and a capacity to influence men. It is worthy of note, moreover, that strong leadership appears most often in an atmosphere of confidence; a defensive mood makes the task of becoming a leader enormously more difficult.

Despite the successes in the economic field, negative accents dominate current analyses. Voluntary organizations in this field—the Committee for Economic Development, the Chamber of Commerce, the Manufacturers Association—as well as the American Federation of Labor and Congress of Industrial Organizations, the United Mine Workers, the Teamsters—all lay stress upon deficiencies, shortcomings, and weaknesses, rather than opportunities. Negativism is a poor environment in which to develop leaders.

All current analyses seem to be dominated by two concepts which have come to fascinate men's minds during the first half of the twentieth century—planning and security. These two words, neither of which is closely defined, have become the watchwords of this generation. In the dictatorships—black, brown, and red— "Plan" was the key; in this respect, the democratic welfare state flattered the opposition by imitation. Plans in the democracies have been neither so precise nor grandiose, but the root idea is there.

So far as humanists and generalists are concerned, planning means very little, the security is almost a contradiction in terms when applied to them. A plan can allocate resources: money, materials, and unskilled, semiskilled, and, to a moderate extent, skilled technical manpower. In planning it is possible, moreover, to make some projections regarding future needs.

Experience has shown those calculations to be extremely crude. This should not be surprising, for it is no exaggeration to say that ours is a revolutionary age outside the political world far more than in that relatively restricted sphere. The enormous growth of government in all countries and at all levels does not affect the validity of that statement. Since World War II, for example, agriculture has changed so rapidly and drastically as to have upset all calculations. Better seeds, better fertilizers, better machines, and better management have produced astounding results. Yet we see these things, not in terms of triumph, but as problems. The bulging surpluses for which government assumes responsibility clearly show that the presumptions upon which the farm program was founded were wide of the mark. It is not long since there was acute concern because young people were leaving the farms for the cities; now the problem seems to be how to prepare them and induce them to do that very thing. The whole temper in dealing with the most astounding victories over hunger in the entire history of the human race is negative and defensive—the antithesis of a sound environment in which to develop leadership.

Industrial planning is complicated by the development of automation. The new word means the industrial revolution raised to the nth power. All estimates of the manpower of many kinds necessary to industry have been subjected to a sharp revision, and present projections bid fair to become obsolete within a very short time; yet the calculators and the servomechanisms are in their infancy.

It seems reasonably clear that, in a free society, planning can be relied upon almost in inverse ratio to development. It is easier to plan for a static or slowly expanding, rather than an explosively dynamic, society. Where science and technology, research and development are pressed, successive "break-throughs" make earlier calculations seem absurd. But so, also, do external events. Just before the outbreak of the Korean conflict, the government of the United States issued statistics which indicated surpluses—of all things!—of teachers and engineers. Within months the projections relative to engineers were shown to be wildly inaccurate; those relative to teachers almost equally so, though at a slower rate. Changes in working habits also make estimates go wrong; it now takes three nurses to do what it was quite customary for one, or at most two, to do only a few short years ago. The advent of prepaid hospital plans, the burgeoning of health and accident insurances of many kinds have had an additional impact. Every estimate of the planners was made obsolete by social changes as well as by science.

The fact of error in planning is very easy to establish and sometimes relatively easy to explain, at least in part. But it has yet to be realized and appreciated that our two watchwords are always in tension, and often in contradiction. If security is essential, if hazard is to be reduced to a minimum, if even the marginal worker —at whatever level—is to be protected in the specific job he holds, planning cannot be bold, for boldness and security do not go together.

This fact goes far to explain many of our difficulties. The full-crew law retarded essential change in the railroads; security hampered progress and ultimately defeated itself. The teachers' requirements, restrictive practices under the guise of standards, assured us of a shortage of teachers in the name of security. During the depression, engineers, chemists, and many others sought to have government control and enforce licensure—again, "standards" covered a drive for security. The whole apprentice system has broken down; labor sought scarcity as a guarantee of security. The pressure for a shorter working week was only in part resistance to being overworked. The demand for overtime is evidence enough. It was a "spread the work" device and created so much "leisure" as to make that into a new "problem." Early and compulsory retirement and dozens of other devices and practices were launched in the name of security, until old age itself has become a "problem," for which we need a "plan."

But there are significant areas within our society for which planning is impossible and where security is unwise. Who can tell us, and by what powers of divination, how many poets we "need" or how many we could "absorb"? On an efficiency basis, the answer is clearly none. As Archibald MacLeish remarked, "Homer has already sung." A vast wealth of poetic literature is lying virtually unused. Some of it has intense beauty, extraordinary insight; it matches thought with cadence in a way to enhance both. If planning is to supply "felt needs," it is clear that millions feel no need, and, so far as reading or listening is concerned, there is already plenty of poetry for every man's lifetime.

It seems perfectly evident that if we are to have poets, it must be upon some basis other than public need or utility. It is part of the record of our society that poets are not always appreciated in their own day and generation. As with other artists, some achieve fame and rich rewards, material and immaterial, during their lifetime. But the general rule runs the other way. Should we plan on producing poets for our unborn generations? Any planner would denounce that proposition as arrant nonsense.

Even assuming utility of poets from a social point of view, how train them, and in what numbers relative to the population? Here we run into a difficulty which even the totalitarians with their tight controls have so far found insuperable. It is possible to make some identification of some sorts of talent at a reasonably early age. All the qualifications in that sentence are important. For no one knows how many men have been lost to professions for which they had substantial talents because they developed slowly, were "late bloomers," and so were not chosen at eleven or twelve to get the education they could have used. Under most systems of education it is at those ages that the sheep are divided from the goats. What skills have been lost by faulty choices we cannot know. At the other end of the scale all who have been engaged in education are familiar with the talented boy or girl who never matures, whose precocity never fulfills its promise. What social pressures, physical weakness, moral deficiency, or any one or a combination of a number of other shortcomings halted development we may know without being able to overcome, or we may never know.

Where there are ability and will and resources, skills may be developed. A man can be trained as a fairly good engineer, at some level, by the expenditure of time and effort. He may make only a fair draftsman, or a satisfactory calculator, or succeed in routine design as a "handbook engineer." Or he may have imagination in addition to skill and knowledge and do wonderful things. We know that under Soviet rule many people are directed or "guided" into occupations they did not select; many others are trained in vocations, more or less voluntarily entered upon, yet they would like to change. Having once been channeled, however, they may not escape over the banks of the stream carrying them onward.

But I never heard of making a poet by training alone. The poetic equivalent of the engineering draftsman is a failure. More training may polish his technique; but if he has nothing to say, no emotional perceptions of a unique kind, skill as a rhymester will still make him no poet. Not all the dictators in the world could order a man, or train a man, to create poetry.

These considerations lead to an absolutely fundamental conclusion which must be accepted by all who would plan our manpower: the only justification for a poet is the poet himself. Utility cannot supply a test. Self-development, self-expression are either valid within themselves, or we should tolerate no poets. For some develop slowly; others achieve recognition slowly. Robert Frost once remarked in my hearing on the instability of his economic status during his first fifty years.

If the poet cannot be manufactured by training or compelled to produce by ukase, and if his gifts, however great, may not be properly recognized, what of security? On the negative side, the answer is easy. The planners may deny him the right of publication. *Dr. Zhivago* could not be published in the Soviet empire; the manuscript had to be smuggled out. His living may be curtailed; Pasternak was denied the fiscal rewards of the Nobel Prize, and probably got little of the royalties earned abroad by his novel. He may be inhibited and stifled—killed, for that matter. But nothing short of death can extinguish the creative spark; the true poet has a compulsion to utter his thoughts, though they be lost in the wind. As nothing in planning, or pressure, or even incentives can produce a positive result from a poetic craftsman who has nothing to say, so none of those things can completely silence one who has much to say.

One fact is very clear. Even the Soviets have had to recognize some of these things as facts of life. As I started to write this paper, one of my first inquiries was how a man became a poet in Russia. It transpired that the word "totalitarian," as so many other words to which we customarily flee—from fatigue with precision—is grossly inaccurate. The inference carried by the word is false. There are vast reaches of life which, although affected, are not controlled even in a dictatorship. If a man wants to be a poet, he may become one. The hazards and difficulties may be severe, but the element of voluntarism remains.

The economy is "planned," but many aspects of experience outside production and exchange are not capable of such close governance. Surely there is not a quota of circus performers, even in Russia; clearly such people are not assigned certain feats to exhibit in the public arena. The element of voluntarism is high in such an area; and, significantly, performance is brilliant.

I have written at some length of poets, but only as an example of all the arts—and, for that matter, the humanities. In thinking about developing leadership for the next generation, those whose predilection is to seek a "plan" will do well to remember that for poets, novelists, essayists, dramatists, actors, painters, sculptors, musicians, historians, philosophers, critics—and all the others who make up the humanistic army—no quotas, no selective service, can achieve a useful end.

Those who would devote their lives to any aspects of the humanities must launch themselves upon their careers by reason of an inner urge. They must have that sense of a call—a vocation —without which no one would face the inescapable hazards. We are aware of and accept the chances taken by the entrepreneur who launches a new business. We are acutely sensitive to the danger of unemployment and have hedged it about with insurances of one kind or another. We too often forget the risk run by a research scientist, and the element of luck in success or failure. Hundreds of men and women may be searching for an effective vaccine and fail to find it while one, whose intellectual gifts, education, and laboratory equipment are no better, hits upon the precise combination which achieves the results so many others sought. A large element of luck—or happenstance, if the word "luck" is offensive—permeates every aspect of life. Nor all the power, nor wealth of the state can alter that stubborn fact.

There is all too little awareness of the innate hazards that are inseparable from the humanities as distinguished from the sciences.

The outlet for them is both a limited and a sophisticated market. Let the planners remember at every step of the way that the more other aspects of life are directed, regulated, and controlled, the more the outlet for humanistic talents tends to shrink. For the market is a voluntary market, and when voluntarism is replaced in any degree by compulsion and control, the loss extends to the receptivity of the public. Whatever pressure is put upon the humanist to conform—for instance, to such as Stalin's dogmas about art and music—the less his crippled work becomes acceptable.

It will be insisted by those who would direct effort more completely that the social hazards are not so marked in a democracy as they are in Russia. That is true; none the less, they may be very severe indeed. Some committees of the Congress in the exercise of their investigative functions have impaired a man's status as an artist for political reasons. Sometimes they have triggered social pressures of a disastrous kind: the blacklisting of writers, producers, and actors in Hollywood is a case in point. Speakers on the floor of the Senate and House of Representatives, under the shield of privilege, have done incalculable harm to men who had no like forum to defend themselves and no right of cross-examination, much less opportunity to produce witnesses in their own defense.

This is an exceedingly sensitive matter for the artist of whatever sort and for the humanist. With all their great contributions to our civilization, which must not be discounted in the least, the scientists, engineers, mathematicians, and production experts are, as specialists, in an essentially neutral position politically. If that were not true, the Union of Soviet Socialist Republics could not have made the giant technological and industrial strides that have characterized its spectacular career over the last forty years. The humanist, on the other hand, has as the heart of his enterprise human values. Inevitably, by the very nature of his commitment and the character of his craft, he must deal with ideas which are politically sensitive. He is guided by values politically dangerous in a planned society. He is not "necessary" to the "giant leap forward"; he is not essential to the economic supremacy to which the Soviets aspire. By the very nature of his work he is expendable, in the sense that even a manual laborer—in a society short of hands —is not.

Whenever, and to whatever degree, a democratic society undertakes manpower planning, the vulnerability of those who deal with ideas is by that measure increased. This truth is partially concealed from us by the unfortunate habit of speaking of free enterprise only as an economic manifestation. Far more significant for the future of democracy is free enterprise of the mind. Vastly more important than economic liberty is freedom to choose voluntarily what one wishes to do, not only for a living, but for a life. Until free enterprise is conceived in these terms—so much broader than the economic—the humanities will suffer, not alone in economic rewards, but in popular estimation, in dignity, in the kinds of distinction which are often more important than the economic security upon which so much stress is laid.

I have been writing of the health, perhaps the survival, of the arts and the humanities. What of leadership? This mysterious quality is not the result of formal training; it is not the fruit of economic reward. If we have many practitioners of the arts, and many scholars devoted to the humanities, the leaders will emerge. Partly it will be the consequence of innate traits; and the characteristics which produce this magic result will be as various as the individuals themselves. To some extent, it will result from environment; there are public moods hospitable to leadership, and others which make it vastly more difficult.

To some degree, it will arise from events. The kind of leader appropriate to one set of external circumstances may find no opportunity for his special brand of leadership in another situation. This is not a counsel of defeat or despair. On the contrary, man is a biological fact. That means, explicitly, that he grows—and decays. Human chemistry is so infinitely complex that the determination of what accelerates and what retards growth is only dimly perceived as yet. We know that growth is not usually steady; it occurs in successive rushes and pauses. The timing of one phase or the other is governed by factors so obscure that we have only the foggiest ideas about them. What is true of all men is peculiarly true of leaders: they grow; they appear; they are supplanted.

It is well in a discussion of leadership to remember that we are governed—whether in a democracy or a dictatorship—by amateurs, who may be regarded as humanists from some points of view, and as generalists par excellence. They are humanists in the sense that they deal with the human situation. In a characteristically provocative essay Lindsay Rogers has quoted Catherine the Great: "You philosophers are lucky men. You write on paper, and paper is patient. Unfortunate empress that I am, I write on the susceptible skins of human beings." They are generalists because the reach of government has now extended so far that no one can be expert in all its phases, or, indeed, in any considerable portion of them.

Those who govern are amateurs in yet another sense. No training course, no education of a formal kind introduces the novice to the art of government. Indeed, very few books are helpful to the practitioner of politics. In this respect, politics is something like teaching: it is an art. It is, therefore, a reflection of the personality of the practitioner. What is amazingly successful for one man is the road to total failure for another. Some work wonders with speech, others with silence; each is astonishingly effective by his own method. Neither could conceivably copy the other successfully.

Moreover, there is no straight road into government. Indeed, few men—very few—start out to be politicians or deliberately plan to make politics their career. There are exceptions, but the usual thing is to get drawn into political action as an avocation and gradually make the transition to full-time absorption. The politician is the perfect example of learning by doing. He can read everything from Plato to Machiavelli to Rexford Tugwell. Reading may give him insights; it may help shape his philosophy of government; but he will get precious few tips on operating.

More than in most other professions, the element of chance plays an extraordinary part in his career. Illustrations are so abundant that every reader can think of his own. The dark horse who comes to the presidency, as did Polk, is one instance. I have seen a man prepare himself to be a senator by entering upon a succession of offices leading to that goal. He was frustrated once because a governor unexpectedly resigned; the lieutenant-governor succeeded and so got in line ahead of the "logical" candidate. So he stood in line, more or less patiently, while the man he planned to succeed refused to retire at a "respectable" age, and seemed destined to live forever. With each passing day, the waiting candidate's chances of ever achieving his cherished goal shrank. Any one of a whole series of accidents could have advanced him, as another series blocked his promotion.

When this element of chance is multiplied by the number of men in the House of Representatives, the Senate, the Cabinet, the Presidency—plus all those who sought those offices—the role of chance is seen to be very great indeed. When all the state offices and municipal offices and those who sought them are added, it is astronomical.

The element of chance continues to play a large part even when the politician attains office. Both Woodrow Wilson and Franklin Roosevelt could easily have been classed as isolationists at the moment they took office. Yet both were forced by events to play great roles in international affairs. Some statesmen have a gift for leading their nation in war. But it has been observed many times that the man who can summon a people to battle and get them to accept all its hardships is often the wrong man to make peace and set policy in peaceful times. The changes on circumstance could be rung indefinitely, and any knowledge of history would be convincing that a planned career in politics is rare, and one that follows the plan with any faithfulness or consistency rarer still.

There are things to do appropriate for the youth who thinks of entering politics. He can read widely in history, in philosophy, and in literature. By that means, he can gain some perspective upon current events; they will lose their novelty, if not their newness. He will find analogues in the past; he will enter vicariously into the experiences of other times, other people, both real and imaginary. He will extend his memory, so to speak; he will stretch his imagination. He will observe that the moral issues remain much the same through the ages; while the circumstances of man alter at astounding speed, his nature changes ever so slowly. He will find relevant answers to present dilemmas in past experience. He will study economics and observe the competing theories. He will also see how seldom practice conforms with any of them.

In sum, he will seek a liberal education and then shape his own life as opportunities and circumstances make possible. Of all occupations for which planning is irrelevant, politics is among the first. How many politicians do we need? Who will set the quota? What will he do when he is out of office? To these and many other questions, there is no simple answer.

Humanists and generalists take years to produce and bring to ripe maturity. To reach this maturity requires personal decision, personal commitment, and readiness to face all the hazards peculiar to the opportunities.

ACHIEVING EXCELLENCE IN
LABOR EDUCATION / *EMERY F. BACON*

IF EVER the labor movement was on trial, it is today. What the eventual outcome will be no one knows. It is the opinion of some that its future no longer dares rest upon the actions and decisions of a few, but will be finally determined by the hopes, aspirations, and the concerted actions of the millions who form its ranks. These members will either resign themselves to a state of inactivity or somnolence in the labor unions with the consequence of further deterioration of labor's influence in our society, or they will insist upon opportunities for self-development and self-expression as free individuals in building a democratic institution for the furtherance of broad social and economic goals in American life.

It has been suggested by some that unions have become too strong, and wrongly use that strength in upsetting the balance of power between government, industry, and labor. Others believe that labor has achieved its maximum growth and influence and is now in a state of decline and stagnation. Still others feel it has never reached its full potential in supporting the liberal tradition. Whatever its actual position is, the role of the individual member will unquestionably be a major factor for positive good or acquiescent lethargy in the years ahead.

For these reasons it is highly appropriate that we consider the thought of achieving excellence in labor education. After all, there can be but little argument that the fate of labor rests primarily upon the information and intelligence of its members and how they are permitted to use both.

Labor education has been relatively slow in developing. It has not been supported either with the enthusiasm or with the money it deserved. Not only have most unions been unwilling to render it the assistance required for mature growth, but also those institutions devoted to education—namely, the universities—have been hesitant and frequently reluctant advocates. As a result, labor education today suffers from a lack of fixed goals, some mediocrity in administrative direction, and frequently unimaginative and sterile teaching. The end product of this sometime underdeveloped and unprofessional educational adventure is a program that has not yet begun to achieve its true potential. I am not unmindful of the significant successes that have been reached in a number of outstanding programs, nor of the expansion and promotion of labor education by a small but dedicated and unusually qualified group of union-university labor educators. But these are the extraordinary situations and their total effect upon most union members is still negligible.

Excellence in labor education has no meaning unless it promotes excellence in the individual. To secure excellence, certain basic assumptions must be agreed upon. First, it must be accepted that while men are entitled to equality before the law, they are unequal in their native capacities and therefore in their attainments. Only by permitting the widest free play to men's differences can there be preserved the freedom to excel which counts for so much in terms of individual aspiration, and has produced so much of man's greatness. Thus it follows that labor educators must be mainly concerned with developing this excellence with due consideration for those differences that exist between people.

It is not necessary here to deal with the matter of purely functional labor education, or to discuss the standards that should be established or the content of the courses offered in the very important tool subjects such as collective bargaining, grievance handling, parliamentary procedure, industrial engineering, and their like. There is a great deal to be said for this type of education, but it must be remembered that the techniques and utilitarian skills of every generation are soon outlived. It is only the verities and the unceasing search for wisdom that pass on from one generation to the next. And so, it is my belief that our concern must be with the problems that perplex us most, even though others loom large on the daily scene.

As we look at American industrial life today in relation to the trade union movement, what are the significant issues that appear? I will not attempt to name them all, but I shall list the several which I believe to be particularly challenging and try to relate their importance to the question of values. The major areas of concern are:

Union democracy. Although there are exceptions, to a remarkable degree democracy does not exist in a majority of American unions. The union movement can hardly be considered a bulwark of freedom and democracy if it stifles the individual rights of its members. Authoritarianism provides scant opportunity for the development or understanding of democracy. The Federal government has recently seen fit to pass legislation requiring an observance of individual members' organizational rights, but how much attention has been paid by labor educators to providing a basis for securing these rights? How many labor education programs for members and staffs have focused attention on individual rights and democratic procedures for all members in the labor unions?

Corruption. To even the most casual observer it is apparent that corruption is deeply buried in the industrial and political life of America. One could scarcely expect the union movement, which is so interwoven with the political and business life of America, to be untainted. But should not one of the purposes of the labor movement be to establish a code of morality and ethics which is not generally found in the market place? The recent findings of the McClellan Committee revealed a portion of the sordidness that has pervaded union life. Even though the revelations touched only a small portion of union leaders and, interestingly, hardly any rank and file members, responsibly informed union officials know that "but for the grace of God" hundreds of others might have been similarly exposed. What role have labor educators played in developing a sense of ethical responsibility among the officers and members of the labor movement? How frequently have values been taught? When and where has major emphasis been placed upon intangible but all-important moral principles?

Politics. What happened to the unsurpassed labor victories of 1958, and what is likely to happen to the liberal sweep of 1959? Or were they liberal sweeps? Have over fifty years of political neutralism originally advocated by that simple man, Samuel Gompers, enslaved the union movement to eternal vassalage under an indistinguishable two-party political system? There is no segment of American society less represented in the legislative, administrative, and judicial life of our country. A major mythology has been built around the subject of union power in politics. The mythology not only solidifies the realistic opposition of the conservatives, but also fragments the vote of the working, the white-collar, and the liberal classes. The net result is that even with frequent victories at the polls there is no substance to the victory in terms of meeting and solving pressing social and economic problems. In almost every state the political organizations are controlled by a combination of industrial, agricultural, and professional politicians. Labor is invariably excluded from their councils and sought only as a fund source and vote promoter. The consequences are few labor candidates for office and fewer honors in appointive positions. How far have labor educators been willing to go in arousing members and groups with allied interests to enter into the stream of political life? How much direction and instruction has been given to union members in solving the problems of housing, medical care, poverty, education, metropolitan planning? No one has a greater interest in these troublesome questions that touch the lives of all workers, but no group has less to say in determining their solution. Why does labor education face this social challenge with only half the interest it displays in the purely functional aspects of trade union life?

Industrial Relations. The stereotypes of the past must be discarded. Too frequently, labor unions and industries are committed to hanging on to the solutions to industrial problems found some twenty years ago. Clauses, contracts, and constitutions written ten, fifteen, and twenty years ago govern an industrial machine that has revolutionized itself during the same period. Wage clauses still set minimum rates of pay frequently supplemented by immoral and antiquated incentive or production rates. Hours of work are relatively unchanged, though hundreds of thousands of workers have been relegated to idleness because of the rapid introduction of automated machinery. The introduction of this new machinery has reduced the physical and sometimes the mental effort required; but instead of labor and management jointly accepting this substitute for human toil and utilizing it for broad humane purposes, frequently its use is permitted to become a point of serious controversy. In the handling of grievances and the settlement of cases by arbitration, the old standards prevail. How much thought has been given by labor educators to straightening out the problems inherent in our grievance procedure? Cannot some better way be found to prevent grievances, rather than bicker over the ways to settle them. Must men incessantly battle for economic justice and insist upon the preservation of shopworn contract issues: the former, which they sometimes consider of less importance than the job, old age security, and modest social amenities; or the latter, which often are simply relics of an earlier age? I believe it to be the responsibility of labor education to point out new ways to secure just economic and social objectives; but more important, to offer ways for labor and management to survive as independent, free agencies in the solution of their problems. It is late. It now seems likely that the economic strife between industry and labor may result in the government legislating ways for problem-solving in the future. It now seems possible that third parties with government fiat may mediate, recommend, or even arbitrate labor-management problems in the years ahead. This could be control of the kind to stifle the imagination of unions and to circumscribe the role they have played in raising living standards and providing countervailing power for big business. How far has labor education gone in probing these areas, and what have been taught as new solutions?

Whitney Griswold, President of Yale University, in his book, *Liberal Education and the Democratic Ideal*, states most perceptively: "During the past century the average working week of our industrial and white collar workers has shrunk from seventy to less than forty hours. The millions of man hours thus conserved form the new Colossus. This Colossus has more leisure at his disposal than all the aristocrats of history, all the patrons of art, all the captains of industry and kings of enterprise. What will he do with it? Will he read? Will he make himself a full man and an exact man, or will he be content to be merely a ready man— a measure of muscle and a shout from the mob? The choice lies before him. Who will help him make it?" My answer to Dr. Griswold would be, "I hope the professionals in the field of labor education will."

Why so much concern with this problem? There are two reasons. First, the survival of a free society requires that men be prepared for it, and that its custody no longer be placed in the hands of a relatively few educated elite. Second, it is the responsibility of educators, as has always been the case—and in our circumstances, labor educators—to fight with stubborn tenacity to secure and maintain the rights of all union members.

In the analytical monograph that B. C. Roberts wrote on *Unions in America,* he comments on the social aspects of unions. He says, "It is frequently suggested that one of the factors causing American unions to become corrupt is their lack of a social philosophy and the decline in their zeal. . . . The rejection of social unionism (i.e., through Gompers' accepted philosophy) in favor of business unionism necessarily involved embracing the ethics of business-elevating materialism, maximizing the return on the dollar, putting acquisitiveness before brotherhood and the achievement of a socially superior society.

"That this type of unionism has been functionally successful is obvious, but it has now reached a state of development where it is faced with a serious challenge. When the wages of millions of workers were extremely low, when millions of workers had no jobs, and the vast majority of them were not even organized, the unions had tremendous giants to slay. They had objectives that transcended any narrow concept of personal, materialist ambition; they were fighting for social ideals, and for the betterment of man and his society. Now that these things have been largely achieved, where, the question may be asked, are the unions to obtain the moral dynamic that is required to defeat corrupting cynicism?"

I wish to quote further. In referring later to non-materialistic goals, Mr. Roberts continues: "Why should the unions concern themselves with matters that are of interest to 'eggheads'? There can be little doubt that this appeal evokes a tremendous response from a society in which a majority of members are ill-educated, narrowly experienced, and feel insecure. The fight for the soul of the American labor movement will not easily be won for enlightenment and the nobler aspects of life, but the great response to the McClellan Committee's request for information about undemocratic and corrupt union practices, which came in letters from thousands of rank-and-file members, at once suggests that there is a latent hunger for honest, democratic unionism that could be encouraged by the resolute leadership of good men."

I have attempted to indicate what the problems are. The next step, then, is to determine what must be done and how to do it. I suggest it be done through the achievement of excellence in labor education.

It seems to me that we have erred in believing that even noble institutions can succeed unless those individuals who compose it have found nobility themselves. A university is considered only as learned as the scholars that form its faculty. A state is only as democratic as its citizens are free. A union is only as valuable in balancing concentrated industrial power with democratic actions as its members have free exercise of individual determination and participation in group decisions.

Labor education, to achieve the excellence we all want, must provide for the individual an opportunity to achieve the full fruition of his moral and intellectual powers so that he may exercise these to his greatest freedom and happiness and the greater benefit of his fellow men.

I quote again from Dr. Griswold: "But if power becomes too concentrated in a corporation or a union and its members are coerced into submission, or if either assumes and selfishly exploits a monopolistic position regardless of the public interest, the public safeguards of individual freedom are weakened by analogy, often by direct influence. Tyranny is tyranny, no matter who practices it; corruption is corruption. If citizens get used to these things and condone them in private affairs, they school themselves to accept and condone them in their public affairs."

The time has come to take another look at the roles that the group and the individual must play in our life, and in the attainment of desirable goals. Obviously we need mass organizations, as represented by the myriad groups that pepper our social fabric.

The groups provide a common meeting place, a shelter, a method of conference, and both a defensive amalgam and an offensive bastion in controversy. But we must realize that little if any creative importance, either in concrete or abstract ideas, has ever sprung from groups. Ideas, inventions, policies, poems have always sprung from the individual. Instead of squelching the imagination, the ideas, the divine spark of reason in people by subordinating them to the crushing power and weight of mass groups, we should be cultivating and drawing out their talents.

The battle between large powerful groups alternately oppressing and dominating the individual, and the individual striving for full expression and freedom has long been waged. In the labor movement there has never been a time when a victory for individual rights and expression was so vitally needed. On the other hand, in our complex society with its interlocking claims upon the person, some forms of organization are not only desired but indeed most necessary. But these organizations, including both labor unions and corporations, should not be exempt from the principles of individual freedom as they were written into the Constitution of the United States.

The low moral standards in America have appalled many people. The continual revelations of persons in both high and low places being bought and sold have a harrowing effect upon all of us. The use of power and money to force conformity and to destroy integrity has risen to a new high. The presumed attainment of collective security from foreign or internal foes has forced us to trade in our individual rights and our creative powers. The securing of material comfort and success has been accepted as a suitable reward for the sacrifice of individualism. Conformity to majority position, whether right or wrong, has become standard procedure.

It is my belief that education provides the instrument by which people discover their capacities and by which they are taught how to develop and use them. Of course, all education won't do this—and that is why we must turn more and more to the type of education which does. What is needed is an education which emphasizes and nurtures both the creativity within an individual and his maximum potential for developing it. It should likewise be directed toward freeing him from the restraints which modern life has placed upon him.

I would not pretend that I have the solution to the problems which I have cited. I am also certain that whatever I suggest will be deemed as frivolous by some, controversial by others, and downright repugnant by many more. The schooled but the uneducated will be among the first, the timorous and the unadventuresome among the second, and the hopeless anti-intellectuals among the third. But there will be support from some, and it is my conviction that this support, though today modest, will eventually gain broad backing and literally change the face of labor education as we know it. From a purely functional approach to the needs of the trade union movement, there will be an evolution that gradually will give dominance to the individual and recapture the moral and social significance of the labor movement.

Three ingredients go to make up excellence in education. They are, in their importance: the instructors, the materials taught, and, finally, the type and length of courses offered. Granted that labor education administrators would find this field both stimulating and rewarding, and would be anxious to develop and adapt programs to meet the needs, there remains the major problem of the instructor and his selection. Superior teachers must be continually recruited, and, the seasoned, learned and skilled teachers must be used more effectively. There is no reason why unions and universities cannot insist upon the highest professional standards for the person entrusted with workers' education. Only rigid adherence to this principle will secure proper professional recognition.

There are books and materials that could prove interesting and worthwhile to workers. The range is wide, and untapped riches lie ready for use. The words and wisdom of the past offer, in infinite variety and understandable terms, some of the answers to the questions which confront us. I have witnessed workers stirred by their first realization of what individual freedom means with the reading of the Declaration of Independence and the Bill of Rights. Others achieve a new dignity when they begin to grasp the challenging words from the old world of Aristotle, Plato, Voltaire, Rousseau, Adam Smith, and Priestley; and from the new world of Jefferson, Franklin, Davis, and Conant. Frost, Hemingway, and Huxley have offered clues to some of the moral problems that men everywhere must face. Their reading has, I believe, brought into sharper focus the values that men live by. Where possible these authors and others should be read and discussed by those who have adequate preparation.

What are the best procedures for providing this type of education? Experiments have now been tested in winter classes, conferences, and summer institutes. All have offered different approaches to the educational purpose and, generally, have accomplished rewarding results. The one general criticism has been that time allotted has been too short. This is a common fault to be found with most education programs for workers.

Since the problems of men in our industrial society are so pressing, and the needs of labor members and staff so acute, either a bold step must be taken to expand and extend labor education in the immediate future, or the cause for which we stand may again be set back for years. I propose, therefore, that the following be considered in order to bring excellence to labor education:

Existing programs operated by unions or by universities, or those operated cooperatively by both, should be re-examined in light of present needs. These programs should retain the basic functional courses usually described as "bread-and-butter," with special emphasis for the new member to acquaint him with his role or job responsibility within the union, and provide him with an understanding of the labor movement, its history, its reason for being, its purposes, and its goals. But, in addition, courses should be offered dealing with the individual and his responsibility for decision-making in a political, social, and economic environment. These courses would, in effect, be concerned with education for freedom.

Four labor education academies, national or regional in scope, and designed to conduct courses for trade union personnel on a year-round basis, should be established. These labor academies would operate residence programs lasting from six to eight weeks for members of labor unions, and conduct conferences and experimental or demonstration programs of a shorter duration. In addition, the academies would develop a full-time staff of professionally trained labor education administrators and instructors. The instructors should be particularly qualified in handling courses dealing with the development of the individual and the issues of humanism and freedom, as well as capable of teaching the basic labor education subjects. Finally, the academies would prepare materials, establish libraries, and develop audio-visual aids useful in their courses. Above all, however, they would provide for a continual review and understanding of labor union democracy, ethics and morals, dynamic industrial relations, desirable social and economic objectives, and international affairs.

There are those today who say it can't be done. This was said for many years whenever the subject of labor education arose. Fifteen years ago there was scarcely anything offered in this field. The University of Wisconsin was the only university that sheltered a labor program then, but it was vastly different from its present program. From a rather recent and modest beginning, labor programs are taught to thousands annually in universities from coast to coast. Most unions, in addition, now either have education departments or participate in general labor education activities.

Not only can such a program as I suggest be created, but I venture to say it will be created. Funds can be secured for it. Buildings will be erected and faculties and staff will be provided. There are scarcely any reasons why we don't have full-time residential programs now, except that no one has tried. Excellence in labor education can be achieved; indeed, it must be achieved. I hope the day is not too far distant when we will devote a major part of our time and effort to developing the talent of individual workers. The Rockefeller Report on Education, known as "The Pursuit Of Excellence," has summed it up very well. It states: "We do not wish to nurture the man of great talent and evil purpose. . . . In short, we will wish to allow wide latitude in the choice of values; but we must assume that education is a process that should be infused with meaning and purpose; that everyone will have deeply held beliefs; that every young American will wish to serve the values which have nurtured him and made possible his education and his freedom as an individual."

To be worthy of the trust placed in us and to secure our common goals, I suggest we alter our course—redirect our steps to provide a fuller and richer education program for workers. It deserves a try and could possibly recapture the imagination and devotion of the millions of hopeful union members.

THE DANGERS OF CORPORATE ACTIVITY IN POLITICS / ARNOLD H. MAREMONT

I PROPOSE to speak of politics. I speak as a businessman who has taken an active interest in politics since 1933, but as one who has never run for public office or been appointed to one. I speak as one who has learned, by experience, that political action has its own rewards in the good men and good causes it supports, without regard to the rewards of office. My remarks, I believe, are applicable to any political party or action.

My purpose is to explain why business, instead of getting into politics, should for its own good stay out. I favor the widest possible participation in politics on an *individual* basis; it is when politics becomes the province of the elite few that I fear for the safety of our system. It is when corporations begin running political classes, conducting political schools, and urging that their executives enter the political arena to expound the corporation viewpoint that I become deeply fearful of the consequences.

The contest over business's part in politics has been going on since Jefferson and the Physiocrats rebelled against the Hamiltonian concept that politics and government should primarily serve business interests. In three distinct periods of our history, the Hamiltonian concept has held sway, and in each instance business has paid a heavy price for its political activity.

The first period was when the Bank of the United States flourished, buying and bribing its way to influence and power. The Jacksonian revolt, which shattered the bank, produced the most profound shocks to the business community. The second period followed the Civil War when the Jay Goulds, the Jim Fisks, and other manipulators played high-wide-and-handsome with the railroads, oil companies and banks, and extended their political influence to the White House itself. Ultimately, their tactics resulted in the Stockyards Act, the Interstate Commerce Act, the Pujo investigation of the "money trust," the Sherman Act, the Clayton Anti-Trust Law, and Federal Reserve regulation of banking and credit. The third period occurred after World War I when Warren G. Harding's "return to normalcy" ushered in an era of unconcern for the social effects of excesses and breaches of trust in the business community. These excesses resulted in the Securities and Exchange Act, the Public Utilities Holding Company Act, the creation of the Tennessee Valley Authority and the Rural Electrification Administration, the strengthening of interstate commerce laws, the rewriting of the Railroad Act, and a host of other New Deal business regulations.

With these observations in mind, I am profoundly convinced that this present campaign to inject business—as business—into politics is ill-conceived, extremely dangerous, a violation of our sound democratic system, and—even worse—perhaps illegal. It seems to me that this kind of political participation may produce a catastrophe rather than create a congenial climate for business. To say the very least, it is hardly a fundamental part of the American Way, and ultimately, it may cast a Marxist shadow over all.

Government exists to assure every individual "life, liberty and the pursuit of happiness," meaning safety of person, the traditional freedoms of speech and worship, equal opportunity, and more recently—since the passage of Social Security and the Employment Act of 1946—a job while he can work, and security when he is old. On the other hand, the corporation's responsibility is not primarily to all people; it must use wisely its investors' money, produce goods and earn a fair profit, treat its employees humanely, and show a just concern for the general welfare.

The areas where the responsibilities of government and business coincide have been expanding, it is true; but wide gaps between them are still evident. Business frequently resists legislative programs which government has determined to be "in the public interest." The business interest is often much narrower than

the public interest. Business's viewpoint is directly influenced by
the effect the proposed program will have on private profit. Its
viewpoint is narrowed by its own immediate concerns. Therefore,
in the past, business has fought against the enactment of the
Pure Food and Drug Act, the Clayton Anti-Trust Act, the Tennessee Valley Authority, Social Security, the Public Utilities
Holding Company and Securities and Exchange Acts, the minimum wage, workmen's compensation, public housing, federal
power regulation, reciprocal trade programs and many other
public policies. It would be interesting to speculate about where
we would be today if business's opposition to these "public interest"
measures had prevailed. I venture the opinion that we could not
function without them.

The corporation is not a political entity; it is a legal entity. It
was never intended to be a political entity. It is wholly different
from the human entity which is the foundation stone of our
Declaration of Independence and our Constitution. In these documents—particularly in Sections 8, 9 and 10 of Article I and in all
of the Amendments—the word "corporation" is not used once.
Corporations were vested with "personality" by a twist given to
the language of the 14th Amendment by conservative majorities
of the Supreme Court in their interpretation of the words "nor
shall any State deprive any person of life, liberty, or property,
without due process of law." The Supreme Court, not the makers
of the Constitution, said that meant corporations, too.

Let us consider briefly the Marxist implications of business
activity in politics. Economic determinism is the foundation of
the materialistic ideology of Communism. With this philosophic
base, Communism's political framework, by design, is totalitarian
—as it must be in order to direct, shape, and control economic
forces.

Those who would project the corporation into politics are
playing directly into the hands of economic determinism. When
the modern corporation becomes hopelessly enmeshed in politics,
we will be well on the way toward economic determinism. Inevitably, as in Russia, this will lead to totalitarianism, the destruc-
tion of our free political heritage, the prostitution of free citizenship and democratic principles. For this reason, I regard the

separation of business from politics as important to our political health as the separation of church from state.

I have recently returned from a trip through the Soviet Union. There, economic determinism holds the factory and the factory worker, the collective farm and its operators in an iron grasp. Everything is geared to the material benefit which the state may reap from the production of goods and money wealth. The Russian system violates all moral concepts of total good and human values. I fear that we will fall into the same deterministic trap if we allow the projection of the corporation into politics. If this should happen, it would not be long before, as in Russia, we all accepted "the word" from on high, and discovered that we had denied the concept that man is many personalities of which the businessman is only one.

Why do corporations want to engage in political activity? One reason is the sometimes hysterically expressed need for a counterforce to the activities of labor in government. Another is the opinion that, since government cannot stay out of business, it has become necessary to influence government in behalf of business interests. How valid are these reasons?

I do not believe that labor and management are locked in a death struggle. Management is charged with earning the maximum profit; and businessmen seem to be doing very well under competitive pressures and the laws and regulatory bodies set up to protect consumer, investor, and labor. Labor, on the other hand, is charged with getting the best deal it can on wages and working conditions. I have never heard responsible union leaders argue that labor ought to engage in politics for the purpose of "clobbering" business. I think anyone who argues that business must get into politics in order to take a poke at labor is doing a distinct disservice to himself, his company, and his country.

I should like to raise here several questions which should be answered by those who would involve business institutions in politics. Under the law, it is well established that a corporation cannot do indirectly what it is forbidden to do directly. How then, being forbidden to contribute money to political campaigns, can a corporation legally permit its employees, on company time and paid by company funds, to act as poll watchers, vote-getters, precinct captains, and such?

If business gets into politics, how can we prevent the development of those very factions which Madison described in the great 10th Federalist Paper—"a landed interest, a manufacturing interest, a moneyed interest, with many lesser interests"? Who would settle the policy contests when all of these interests begin their inevitable struggles for supremacy in government?

If a business organization enters the political arena, who would choose the party which will be favored with its support—the directors, the shareholders, the chairman of the board? Where does the company find authority to use shareholders' money for such purposes? Will not the employees who belong to different organizations, unions, or political parties develop a profound antagonism for the corporation's political activities? Seeing the officers use company funds and time for political action, will they not sharpen their own demands and opposition?

What will be the effect upon the customers of the corporation who are also of many political persuasions, and interests—who are property owners and renters, union members and white-collar workers, protagonists or antagonists of myriad causes and ideas?

The American people have, with comparative equanimity accepted bigness in our corporations. A. A. Berle, in his Fund for the Republic study, "Economic Power and the Free Society," reports that 50 per cent of American manufacturing is held by 150 corporations; and two-thirds of the economically productive assets of the nation—excluding agriculture—are held by 500 corporations. Business firms have become so big that they "can be thought of only in somewhat the way we have heretofore thought of nations," Mr. Berle states. Most people are not greatly disturbed by this. But when you try to tell them that "what is good for General Motors is good for the country," you have a real row on your hands!

Is it inevitable that our heritage of democratic politics be lost while we give lip service to it and perfect our manufacture of the organizational man? This man, as William H. Whyte, Jr., and David Riesman have shown in their studies, is not particularly suited to bold imagination, bold thinking, bold concepts of the public welfare, and mass cooperative action and leadership on the political stage.

George Romney of American Motors recently commented on this problem in strong language: "We have corporate executives and white-collar employees who have become political eunuchs and who have substituted corporate citizenship and the hope of economic advancement for their priceless heritage of independent political action."

Andrew Hacker of Cornell University, in his paper on "Politics and the Corporation" says: "The Corporation has certainly not set out to weaken the foundation of democratic politics, but its growth as the characteristic institution of our time is having this consequence."

The "Corporation Man," Mr. Hacker points out in his remarkable paper, ordinarily does not own property. He is highly mobile, shifting from one section of the country to another. He tends to substitute corporation virtue and corporation thinking for civic virtue and ardor. He is careful to do and say the things that will be found pleasing to his superiors and that will lead to his promotion. He will participate in such safe ventures as the American Red Cross and Community Fund drives, not necessarily because of personal zeal, but because "the company expects it."

"It would be wrong to say merely that the middle-class corporation employee is afraid to join in," says Mr. Hacker. "It is rather that he has neither the interest nor the inclination to identify himself with politics. . . .

"The middle-class, in divorcing itself from politics and in making itself dependent on the largesse of corporate institutions, has weakened itself immeasurably. If a crisis arises, even a relatively mild one, can we be sure that this group will continue to adhere to democratic values?"

Parenthetically, it should be observed that studies of the new suburbia, where the organization man mostly resides, show, according to Hacker, that "the incidence of neurosis, the conflict in values, and the feeling of helplessness are endemic; a sense of isolation and powerlessness is having profound social and psychological effects on the members of the middle class."

These are not the qualifications for successful participation in politics. Corporation thinking and corporation training destroy the very imaginativeness and bold action that is so often required in politics. Alan Harrington states in his book, *Life in the Crystal Palace:* "Once upon a time free enterprise invoked the principle of the survival of the fittest. Today at the Crystal Palace we have the survival (or rather the promotion) of the most imitative . . .

"In surveying his team, almost any executive is going to appraise it so that the men below who might challenge his method of doing things will be put in their proper places. . . .

"I suspect that most jobs in a corporation and elsewhere can be mastered in a few months, or at any rate in a year or two. What cannot be learned that quickly is the corporation minuet—the respectful dance with the right parters. The watchful corporation man gradually finds out who is important and who is not, what is acceptable and what is not, what type of project will advance his fortunes and what is not worth bothering about. Experience for him mainly adds up to learning how to behave. The secrets of gauging and responding to the power of others—superimposed on a normal intelligence—will move him slowly upward."

Authors Whyte and Riesman have drawn graphic pictures of the nature of the organizational man, the erasure of his personality, his avoidance of any semblance of controversy such as is the life of politics, his removal from the individuality, experimentation, and non-conformity which is also the life of politics. Furthermore, these men avoid anything that may inject elements of controversy between themselves and their superiors.

Suppose that Company X is politically active through Mr. Raymond Jones, its first vice-president. Suppose Mr. Jones is, in due time, inspired with the public interest and wants to run for Governor, not without excellent prospects of success. Suppose that he strongly believes in a better school system, better teaching facilities, and more adequate pay for teachers. Suppose that he proposes to raise the money for better schools by increasing corporation franchise or profits taxes? What do you think will be the attitude of Company X? And if Mr. Jones persists, how long do you suppose he will be first vice-president of Company X?

The organizational man is not going to make his political activity an area of controversy with his chiefs. What they decide to espouse may or may not be good for the company, or for the public interest, but they write his pay checks, and it is not up to him to bite the hands that wield the pen.

Is it necessary to accept the corporation as our characteristic institution and develop a mould that makes a pallid, faceless human of its employees, substituting impersonal corporate interest for personal interest? I do not believe the problem is that desperate. Our democratic system protects the individual's right to exercise his franchise freely and secretly. The emphasis is on the *human* rather than the legal being. We vote as humans—not as employer, employee, father, homeowner, renter, taxpayer, or what have you. Classify us as you will, code us, punch us into cards, write us into impulses in Univac—we will emerge as humans, enjoying and exercising our right "to be different" which is the great force of life as remarked by Michel de Crevecour nearly two hundred years ago. It was Thomas J. Watson who said, "All great questions of politics and economics come down in the last analysis to the decisions and actions of individual men and women. They are questions of human relations, and we ought always to think about them in terms of men and women—the individual human beings who are involved in them."

The modern corporation, equal in size and power to many of our states, as Mr. Berle has shown, is not set up to think or act in terms of the individual. In fact, it serves to repress and stifle the individuality and the other qualities that are essential in politics. A corporation is an amalgam of a great many personalities, divided into categories of importance, directed from the top by persons who have prejudices as violent as you will meet anywhere. They are the ones who have set out to provoke, to stimulate, and to encourage business participation in politics. They are not men without judgment; they have a lot of judgment, and they know exactly what they are after.

As individuals, these men have every right—as does any employee—to harbor an opinion as citizens of a democracy. They can be as enlightened or benighted as their natures and their minds permit. But they have absolutely no right to use corporation machinery, corporation money, and corporation personnel to inflict their views upon other individuals or upon the community.

Under our system, the one time when man is absolutely free is when he enters the polling booth; but he is *not* free if he is told by the corporation which employs him to go out and ring door-bells, make speeches, distribute literature and propagandize the corporation views. No company has the right to use its economic power and influence to dragoon its members into political action.

The argument that corporations can conduct company classes in politics and public service without influencing the personal views of their employees is naive. The influence of the corporation exists like the pressure of the atmosphere—15 pounds to the square inch. Actually, the corporation is training the executive to teach the corporate viewpoint. The assertion that these courses are directed toward "local politics"—that is, toward the aldermanic races and similar small fry offices where party labels and ideological designations play no part—is false and misleading.

To be politically effective, an employee has to begin by affiliating with a party. There is no other way of doing the job. He then becomes the protagonist of the general ideology and orientation of his party. Party labels *do* mean something; they mean very much to the men who head corporations. As Professor Stephen K. Bailey points out in his fine study, "The Condition of our National Political Parties," there is a difference: "The Democratic party basically is a party of innovation, with a 'pro-government' bias. The Republican party is an essentially consolidating party with a limited-government bias." The corporation employee who is projected into politics faces, quite often, the problem of submerging his own political convictions because economically he cannot afford to be openly unsympathetic to the policies and purposes of the corporation.

When a corporation "teacher" asks his class, "How did your Congressman vote on the right-to-work bill?" or "How did your Senator vote on Reciprocal Trade?" his so-called "students" could hardly be oblivious to the political implications and bias of his questions.

The corporation has no altruistic desire to render selfless and perhaps sacrificial public service. *It has an axe to grind.* That axe is the desire to advance the business ideology of the corporation by projecting "hired hands" into political party action, after they have been sufficiently indoctrinated. Many companies have decided that what is wrong with the world is that their executives are inactive in politics, or if active do not identify themselves with and propound the corporate viewpoint in party councils. They want to inject the views, prejudices, opinions, and sometimes the bias of management into political considerations.

There are ample means of getting the business viewpoint across, without entangling business in politics. There are advertising pages and radio and television time which can be bought; there are such groups as the American Medical Association, U.S. Chamber of Commerce, Farm Bureau Federation, National Association of Manufacturers, AFL-CIO and a thousand others engaged in promoting and advancing special viewpoints and policies; and, finally, the editorial pages of most of our magazines and newspapers are generally sympathetic to the business viewpoint. I do not feel, as a businessman, that I am prevented from getting the business viewpoint before the public.

I suggest that if corporations want their executives to be trained in politics, they let the schools and colleges do the job. Why don't they take the funds they spend on company classes, turn them over to a college, and let the college teach political courses for executives? Most colleges would welcome the opportunity. But no, the corporations run their own classes because they want to *control* what is taught.

If a company wants to encourage political participation, let it contribute to the American Heritage Foundation and other organizations which specialize in political education and getting out the vote. Many corporations don't take this course, because they want to inject the corporation viewpoint into whatever political activity they undertake.

I think that it is equally outrageous for corporations to dole out money as gifts to universities and colleges. These donations, in too many cases, represent an effort by the directors to inject their views and the corporation policies into the educational processes, where they do not belong. It is bad in principle, bad for education, and bad for the company. There is now far too much corporation and government influence in education through the issuance of grants, donations, and research allowances.

I believe that it would be much better if a central agency were established to which (and only to which) corporations might make educational donations. Such an agency would then pass the funds along to the colleges and universities that need them, without passing along at the same time a large dose of corporation influence and policy.

Even though I believe strongly that business should stay out of politics, I believe equally strongly that individual businessmen, as citizens, can and must assume their share of political responsibility. Mr. Paul Butler, the former Democratic National Chairman, said that the individual businesman who ignores politics "does so at his peril, for politics will most certainly not ignore him."

If you accept the premise that we are "all around humans" then it follows that we are "political humans" seeking action through unity of ideals and spirit, not as businessmen, workers, scientists, or as categorized interests. Our responsibility, then, as persons who want to be useful members of society, is to recognize first that politics is power, second that as citizens who can direct that power to the development of the good society, we have a responsibility to help. Power is exercised responsibly through a political party—not through mobs or debating societies. We must participate as active, responsible, articulate individual citizens. It is not for us to judge from Olympian heights, or to stand on the sidelines of political battles. The Greeks had a word for people who avoided politics. The word was "idiot."

Many businessmen talk in generalities and act like the young man in love who wrote to his sweetheart:

"There is nothing I would not do to reach your side. I would climb the highest mountain. I would cross the trackless desert. I would swim the widest ocean to be near your side, my beloved."

"P.S. I'll see you Saturday night if it doesn't rain."

Are we willing to engage in politics, rain or shine? Are we going to be an anvil or a hammer, as Goethe once asked? Are we going to stand aloof in this challenging world, wearing provincial, single-track blinders? Are we going to be like the Englishman who wrote to the headmaster, "Don't teach my boy poetry. He is going to stand for Parliament." Or shall we take the view that if more poets were politicians and more politicians knew poetry we might have a better world?

A recent Harvard Business School Club study states that "there exists a frightening lack of interest in the business community for its participation in the government service" and when business does take an interest "more and more qualified business men are serving constantly shorter periods." The late Justice Arthur C. Vanderbilt of New Jersey once observed that "the antipathy to politics is reflected in the home, the church, and the school." In a recent national poll, it was reported that 69 per cent of those polled did not want their children to enter politics and almost 50 per cent thought that no man could be in politics and remain honest. This is about as sad a commentary as one could imagine.

We *must* recognize that the political party is the only valid means of giving organization, direction, drive, and expression to the public power. We *must* get away from the idea that when we have voted we have done the whole duty of man.

Traditionally, politics, like big league baseball, was played only by the experts. We were permitted to participate by rooting for your side, but not by helping to select the players. All of this has been changed. The primary system does enable us to help pick the players. To be effective, we *must* join the party that most nearly represents our views and supports our kind of candidates. The business of "voting for the man" once every four years and forgetting about party policies in between is utterly foolish.

The businessman in particular has an obligation to join a political party and make his voice heard in party councils. But the business-man who becomes politically active must choose his party as an individual who wears no man's or no corporation's collar. It must be *his* choice. I repeat and emphasize that organized corporate activity with all its subtle innuendoes is not conducive to spontaneous individual participation in political affairs. The business-man must seek out and work with a like-minded group in his township or precinct, for *group action* is the key to success.

It may be that the businessman is not welcomed into the regular party organization. Some of these function as "closed" societies. In the primaries, where only the loyal and dedicated vote, such strangleholds by the few are perpetuated. But if he is not wel-comed by the party organization, there is another way he can be active and influential. That is by joining political clubs of either party, many of which have provided and still provide new blood, new ideas, new vigor outside the regular organizations. Here he will find that the controls are in the membership, not in some remote smoke-filled room.

Stephen A. Mitchell, a former Democratic National Chairman, in his book, *Elm Street Politics,* tells how he organized a club on his block. It is exciting adventure, and it works. As Mitchell points out, the club idea was given great impetus in the 1952 and 1956 elections when the Citizens for Eisenhower and the Volunteers for Stevenson, both groups outside the regular party organization, worked with great energy and effect. In forthcoming elections the balance of political power may well reside with the people who are most attracted by the club organization.

Old-style machine politics are dying out; in 1958 the old line "pros" lost ground in most states, and even a great professional politician like Governor Lawrence of Pennsylvania could not carry his ticket with him. We have rid ourselves of the Hague Machine in New Jersey, the Crump Machine in Tennessee, the Pendergast Machine in Missouri, and a host of lesser political machines in other areas. In my opinion, the worst course business can take is to conduct political action programs which, inevitably, will lead to company machines not unlike those political machines which have passed into limbo. Only if each businessman assumes his political responsibilities as an individual can our democratic heritage be preserved.

SHOULD BUSINESS GO IN
FOR POLITICS? / CHARLES P. TAFT

AMERICANS READ almost daily now that business men should go into politics. This has been said before, but not so often or so broadly. A few years ago, business leaders were being urged to work at the local political level. Now, every salaried employe in some companies is being called upon to select the party that best represents his point of view and work for that party in his neighborhood.

This sounds good, especially to one who has watched local groups seek business-man candidates for, say, the City Council in such a well-governed and progressive city as Cincinnati. The task of finding candidates is harder every year, it seems. Perhaps, one thinks, this movement can help. But how "civic" is it?

Business has been in politics a long time. I have been told that at the end of the seventeenth century the sons of Robert Taft, a wheelwright of Mendon, Massachusetts, became selectmen of the town and worked hard to get a bridge built to the west over the Blackstone River—where, coincidentally no doubt, they owned some land.

Certainly the "robber barons" were in politics up to their ears, from Jim Fisk to Commodore Vanderbilt to the copper kings of Montana. Railroaders, liquor dealers, insurance men, shipping magnates, fair-traders and price discounters are only a few of the business men who have found it necessary to go to State Legislatures and Congress. Makers of fire-department equipment, concrete and blacktop purveyors, clay-pipe manufacturers, road and building contractors all are concerned with who is Mayor, City Manager, Councilman, or Governor.

Companies of any size have a trouble shooter, part or full time, who knows his way around in politics. He may also be the one who decides what campaign contribution is made to what politician by what officer—from his personal salary, of course.

Government regulation in the state or national capital makes a common front essential to an industry. Government contracts may be the lifeblood of the business, as with most airframe companies. So trade associations grow and prosper, and larger companies have branch offices in Washington.

Then what is new about the business-into-politics movement? One thing is its scale. One nationally known corporation has trained a battalion of 500 executives to spread the gospel of company views on public issues. Another new element is that the present movement, upon examination, begins to assume some of the aspects of a public-relations operation. There is even a New York advertising firm organized in 1958 specifically to advise companies in this limited field.

Is all this good or bad? How far will it get?

There is a lot of sound thinking behind a program for a "better business climate." A big local plant is usually a sitting duck for a rabble rouser on a City Council. It shouldn't be; its intelligent leaders—and its employes on lower levels—ought to fight back.

But there is something wrong with the broad drive to get employes into politics. Even the political public relations firm warns business men to look out. Democratic National Chairman Paul Butler, in a joint interview in May of 1959 with Thruston B. Morton, his Republican counterpart, said: "With . . . narrow purposes in mind they are going to end up alienating the general public, creating suspicion of the business community and doing a clumsy job of obtaining even their narrow objectives." And Mr. Morton warned: "If business men are to achieve a maximum effectiveness in politics, they must work toward this goal as citizens rather than as spokesmen for, or representatives of, just one segment of our total economy."

Henry Kaiser and George Romney, both pretty good judges of sound business public relations, have stood against the whole idea of business telling its employes to go into politics—apparently for just the reasons Butler and Morton gave.

That warning is sound. What is really self-interest, however justifiable, ought not to be blown up into civic spirit, and it ought to be advanced with some degree of attractive modesty and humility. What is good for General Motors is not necessarily good for the country—or the city.

A second thing wrong with the campaign is that it is, in fact, aimed at labor. This central motivation—to rival big labor and beat down labor organizations—is openly stated in many cases. An executive of a large corporation, in a speech to the Business Advisory Council in October, 1958, urged more vigorous political action by business men because of his "personal" appraisal of the AFL-CIO as the "most aggressive and successful force in politics." This power, he said, is "principally in the hands of other (than racketeer) union officials, who nevertheless put forth ideologies and proposals which result in inflation, concentration of power in central government, damage to progress and withering of freedom." I cannot remember any endorsement of political participation by business not closely related to emotion about the labor problem.

You may ask why this campaign should not be aimed at labor. There are two good reasons.

One is that labor is not as effective at the polls or in Congress or the State Legislatures as is assumed in this emotional reaction. The Taft-Hartley Act was passed by more than a two-thirds margin over President Truman's veto and the labor reform bill that recently passed the House was certainly not the one labor wanted. At the local level, labor seldom really works *for* a candidate—only once since 1925 in Cincinnati, for example.

Labor can vote *against*, when the issue is something like the "right to work," and when people in general feel the issue is simply punitive, not constructive. And if labor comes out to vote on such an issue, it may knock off a candidate incidentally, as it did Senator John Bricker in Ohio. But although workers may get herded out to register, they do not vote as "labor." In fact, they do not vote much at all. Their local leaders have their hands too full with union politics to spend much time on local, state, or national party politics.

The other reason against just "opposing labor" is that a wholly negative campaign, for all that it may be temporarily effective, does not work in the long pull. As Arthur Motley, the publisher of Parade Magazine and a leader in the successful fight to elect Representative John V. Lindsay against the opposition of the Republican organization in New York's Seventeenth District in November, 1958, has put it: "I can see no future for business and our kind of economy if we're merely going to have 'big business' opposing 'big labor' in the political arena."

This leads to the third general objection to the "business into politics" campaign—the fact that it looks, and sometimes acts, as if it were against all progress. For example, an official of one of our largest corporations, active in the movement, has talked about "successful Republican candidates who were pulled far to the left in their campaign obligations and promises." The head of another company, located in New Jersey, which conducts one of these programs, has been reported organizing to prevent the renomination of Clifford Case as Senator from that state because his record is "indistinguishable from the Americans for Democratic Action." Yet Case in four years is recorded as supporting President Eisenhower 85 per cent of the time, as compared with 83 per cent for former Senator H. Alexander Smith.

There is an interesting schizophrenia here. The National Association of Manufacturers and the United States Chamber of Commerce are officially opposed to any program like public housing, and want urban renewal stopped or reduced rapidly. Yet many of their distinguished members belong to organizations in Pittsburgh, Cleveland, Cincinnati, Boston, or San Francisco which are the civic spark plugs for urban renewal as the only cure for the blight at the heart of practically every large city in America. In that connection they support public housing. They go to state capitals and to Washington and say so, while the N.A.M. and Chamber of Commerce present resolutions to the contrary in the same places.

It may be argued that if business men want to go into politics to oppose labor, urban renewal or Senator Case, that is their privilege. To this I answer that we are talking about politics and that politics, as the art of the possible, is no place for anti-intellectual absolutism about economics and social sciences, or about individuals either. I do not advocate compromise with principles but I do mean that in these areas nobody knows all, that humility learns more than arrogance and that an intelligent and honest opponent may have a little—just a little—in which he may be right.

My final objection to the "go into politics" movement is that it generally neglects local government where public servants provide us with streets, sewers, hospitals, police protection, water and garbage disposal. Rather, the movement's sponsors back the local "organization" for supposedly doing the job for the Republican candidates for President, Senator, Congressman or Governor. (Let us face it: these sponsors work with Democrats because they have to in most large cities, but they are all Republicans.)

The truth is that a local Republican organization does very little for the four named officials on the Republican ticket, especially if there is a real fight on. It is much more interested in the Probate Judge (Surrogate in New York), the Auditor (tax assessor), the Sheriff and the County Commissioners.

My late brother, Senator Robert A. Taft, now highly revered by the organization in Cincinnati, always ran well *behind* those local officials, and it was not the Cincinnati or any other local organization that pulled him through for re-election in 1944 by just 17,000 out of well over 2,000,000 votes in the state of Ohio.

Local government—good, efficient local government—is where any political movement ought to begin, especially when, as today, most national domestic issues, including labor corruption, have their roots there. And from local government, too, come those good candidates for national office whom this movement is looking for.

But few spokesmen for the movement even think of local government when they make their speeches. I heard a top corporation man describe the whole program to a president's round table of the American Management Association. When he had finished I asked if what he said applied (1) to local government, and (2) to a city with an independent local movement like our Cincinnati Charter Committee and (3) to places like Detroit or Dayton where the national parties take no part in local elections. (A poll taken April, 1959, showed that 60 per cent of American cities with more than 50,000 population have no Republican or Democratic activities.) The answer was that, of course, the program applied there, too. I can only say there is very, very little in his company's literature to show it.

Yet there is much that business men could do in politics. They are urgently needed. Clearly, since I have been so critical, it is up to me to lay out some guide lines.

(1) One thing that business men are doing, and that they should do more of, is exemplified by the Cleveland Foundation, the Citizens Development Committee in Cincinnati, and the Allegheny County group in Pittsburgh. These organizations back master plans for their areas, and help and encourage local officials of their party to carry these plans through. Their business-man members go to state capitals and Washington to help cut through red tape or get new legislation.

(2) Business men should take adult courses in economics, as members of the Committee for Economic Development do. Too many of the vocal ones rely on self-constituted research organizations that tell them what they want to hear instead of on professional recognized groups like the National Bureau for Economic Research, the Brookings Institution, or the National Industrial Conference Board.

(3) Business men ought to write their own speeches and do a lot of their own homework. They should practice persuasive speaking, seek critical comments on their technical proficiency. Few business men can stand up to comparable labor leaders, mostly for want of practice and training in both sound economics and public speaking.

(4) Business men who go into politics should learn first that the "pros" have no interest in their participation except as moneybags or fat cats, and perhaps as rubber stamps for the ticket.

To put it affirmatively, the place to begin is usually with a fight —*against* the organization—to get good candidates nominated and elected in both the party primary and the election. Talking about starting in the precincts of your own party organization is eyewash, because intelligent young business men are the last thing the local machine wants. It wants order-takers who will produce votes for the slate at the primary. After that, of course, the voters probably have little choice.

This is not a sorehead's gripe. I can get myself elected in my home town against the organization. I have done it in eleven primary or general elections, and I have lost in only three.

But my point is shown by the White Plains Republican primary fight of a couple of years ago, in which a group of insurgent beginners lost by only 1,000 votes in 20,000, and by the 1958 victory for an anti-organization Republican Congressional candidate in New York's Seventeenth District. A group of young Republican business men has even analyzed the marginal districts around the country and set out to show, with some success, what a good plan can do, with good local leadership.

Every good American ought to be in politics, because through politics his government is run in a way that provides justice for his rights, and the services that make it possible to live as pleasantly as few in history have lived before. Business men can help make the word "politician" an honorable tag, even an intellectual tag, and have all kinds of fascinating fun doing it. But no one should fall for the canned slogan: "Join the party of your choice and start working in it at the precinct level (and, boy, let's sock these damned unions)."

EDUCATION IN ACTION:
ACTION IN GOVERNMENT

MR. TRUMAN'S USES OF
HISTORY / R. G. COWHERD

FORMER PRESIDENT Harry S. Truman made more use of history than most of his predecessors in the White House. Perhaps no other President has drawn more heavily from the storehouse of man's past experience than he did, and certainly none has been more conscious of his reliance upon history in making major decisions. In public addresses and in his published *Memoirs* he clearly acknowledges how he has been instructed and encouraged by the precedents of former Presidents and other great men of the past.

From his early youth, Mr. Truman has been an insatiable reader of history. Beginning with the Henty adventure books and Abbott's biographies of great men, he went on to weightier volumes setting forth man's experience from the earliest written record. He read not merely formal works but also letters, memoirs, newspapers, and other stuff of which the textbooks are made. The lives of famous men and women intrigued him, but the reading of biography was more than the romance of heroes, for he searched the background to find an explanation for their success and failure. His searching for an explanation of the role of great men in history gave him the solid instruction in law and government which he felt he needed long before he thought of entering public life. "I know of no other motivation," he writes in his *Memoirs*, "which so accounts for my awakening interest as a young lad in the principles of leadership and government."

Since "what history taught me" runs like a refrain through the *Memoirs,* I wrote to Mr. Truman to inquire what books had been of greatest value in preparing him for the Presidency. As a teacher of history, I had anticipated that he would point to the standard constitutional histories. But to my surprise he listed the classical studies of other countries and peoples, including Plutarch's *Lives,* Gibbon's *Decline and Fall of the Roman Empire,* Green's *History of the English People,* and Guizot's *France.* These classics supplied a vision of greatness and painted the movement of peoples on a grand scale. Thus it happened that Mr. Truman began his public career surrounded by a great cloud of witnesses. Communion with such companions was his moral education.

The years in Washington as Senator and Vice President gave Mr. Truman occasions to see the White House brilliantly illuminated under its spotlights. He saw it also under the sweeping searchlights of history. The long procession of Presidents moving in and out with their cargoes of responsibilities engaged his sympathies, and their triumphs and failures fired his imagination. His vision of the White House was different from that of the architect who had designed it. The architect saw it as a place for the President to live; Mr. Truman saw it more truly as the Executive Mansion. This exalted vision of the White House caused him frequently to confront himself with, "Harry, what are you doing here?"

Mr. Truman's early training was a strong factor in his gaining the nomination for Vice President. The reading of history had persuaded him that great administrators affect the destiny of people as much as military conquerors. This awareness disposed him to accept those appointments in the Senate entailing heavy administrative duties. Before undertaking an investigation of the war effort, he studied similar proceedings during past wars and discovered that a Congressional committee investigating the conduct of the Civil War had seriously obstructed the military efforts of the federal government. Hence, when he became chairman of the Senate Special Committee to investigate national defense during the Second World War, he strove to avoid "every pitfall into which my predecessors had fallen." His proven abilities in conducting this inquiry brought him to the attention of President

Roosevelt, who suggested his nomination for Vice President in 1944.

While serving as Vice President, Mr. Truman sought to prepare himself for the exigency of becoming President. He searched the careers of his predecessors, especially of those who had succeeded to the higher office, only to discover that the Vice Presidency was not an adequate preparation. He learned from history that the Vice President is nominated as a political person, and if elected he continues to associate with the shrewdest politicians. Since he is in effect a member of Congress, he can never enter fully into the President's confidence, for any premature disclosure of policy, though inadvertent, might seriously hinder the executive branch of government. The realization that he could never adequately prepare himself for the succession to the Presidency filled Mr. Truman with anxiety as President Roosevelt's illness became apparent.

When President Roosevelt died suddenly in April of 1945, Mr. Truman succeeded him in office inadequately briefed for the difficult decisions at hand. He was now Commander-in-Chief of the Army during a World War moving toward its consummation. The flood tide of world affairs bore him swiftly along. The historian Truman, who measured time by the magnitude of his decisions, wrote of this experience: "I felt as if I had lived five lifetimes in my first five days as President."

During the first year in the White House, President Truman studied the aftermath of the First World War seeking to learn from conditions which paralleled his own. When establishing the United Nations, he avoided the mistake of Woodrow Wilson by gaining in advance the consent of congressional leaders and by appointing Republicans as delegates to the San Francisco Conference. If the failures of the League of Nations warned him against a sanguine optimism, the successful federation of the American colonies encouraged him to believe in the ultimate triumph of the United Nations. "I always kept in mind our own history," he said, "and the experience in the evolution of the Constitution. It took many years and a number of amendments to make the Constitution work. It would take years for an international organization to work effectively."

Mr. Truman was too wise an historian to depend solely on tradition as a guide. Though past conditions afforded him instructive parallels, new situations arose which beleaguered his reason for an answer. The decision to drop the atomic bomb was guided by traditional military thinking, but the control of atomic energy in peacetime was without precedent. His sense of history made him aware of the magnitude of this undertaking. "The decisions I had to make . . . on the control and use of atomic energy," he said, "could well influence the future course of civilization."

In foreign affairs Mr. Truman made several decisions which departed from traditional American relations with the rest of the world. His determination to maintain the independence of Greece and Turkey, thus blocking Russia at the Dardanelles, was, in his own words, "a turning point in American foreign policy." Other phases of his policy affecting Europe, the Marshall Plan and the North Atlantic Treaty Organization, were corollaries of the Truman Doctrine to maintain the independence of nations threatened by Communist penetration and Russian military aggression. Mr. Truman's knowledge of history made him sure-footed in European affairs. Perhaps his ignorance of Oriental history, an ignorance shared by most Americans, explains his lack of success in dealing with China.

The Point Four program, another departure in American foreign policy, arose from Mr. Truman's knowledge of American economic history. "I knew from my study of history," he said, "that this country was developed by the investment of foreign capital. . . ."

The Truman foreign policy moved the United States beyond the point of returning to isolationism. But a man with less historical knowledge might have put his head in the noose of the western isolationists, who fondly quoted Washington's farewell address against entangling alliances. Mr. Truman compared the isolationists to preachers who quote Bible verses out of context, for he had learned that doctrines have little meaning apart from the situation in which they are embedded. By relating doctrines to conditions, Mr. Truman became convinced that the growth of the United States had long outmoded Washington's method of making the nation secure.

The making of far-reaching decisions in foreign affairs was Mr. Truman's forte. The faults of procrastination, the bane of most administrators, were never his. His dramatic, swiftly moving career poses questions for the educator. What training prepared him for the making of decisions? How did history, his acknowledged teacher, help him render those decisions which have raised him on a pinnacle among the greatest Presidents? Mr. Truman has given his answer to these questions in his *Memoirs:* "Whether my early interest stemmed partly from some hereditary trait in my natural make-up is something for the psychologist to decide. But I know that the one great external influence which, more than anything else, nourished and sustained that interest in government and public service was the endless reading of history which I began as a boy and which I have kept up ever since."

History endowed Mr. Truman with esteem for those Presidents who had grappled with difficult situations. Increasingly he thought of the Presidency as a decision-making office. This function he stressed in his farewell address. "The greatest part of the President's job," he said, "is to make decisions—big ones and small ones, dozens of them almost every day. The papers may circulate around the government for a while but finally they reach this desk. And then there's no place else for them to go. The President —whoever he is—has to decide. He can't pass the buck to anybody. No one else can do the deciding for him. That's his job." The President's great power to decide questions affecting the welfare of millions of people filled him with awe. "There is no job like it on the face of the earth," he said, "in the power it concentrates at this desk and in the responsibility and difficulty of decisions."

History had prepared Mr. Truman to make difficult decisions by training him to read quickly, widely, and imaginatively. It had taught him to assimilate masses of complex materials which would have baffled anyone unaccustomed to thinking in terms of the movements of people and nations through centuries. The great mass of papers that reached his desk required him to put in seventeen hours a day and to sign his name on the average of 600 times. Little wonder that he thought of himself "as a man on a tiger who must keep on riding or be swallowed."

That Mr. Truman came through the ordeal of the Presidency undaunted continues to astonish his admirers. He retained his fortitude through the trying years because he could sleep on his decisions once they were made. But he did not make them easily. "By nature not given to making snap judgments or easy decisions," he tells us, "I required all the available facts. . . . I trained myself to look back into history for precedents because instinctively I sought perspective in the span of history for the decisions I made. That is why I read and reread history."

Such a reading of history puts a man on the rack. It stretches every fiber. Only a man of great stamina endures the wrenching. Facing crucial questions, he mixes anxiety with knowledge. He calls on his own experience and empties it of guidance. He lives vicariously and draws upon the wisdom of others. Even after diligently probing the past, he may still be in a wilderness, dependent upon his ingenuity and imagination for a way out.

However ingenious a President may be and however subtle his reasoning, there can be no comprehending of public affairs without a sense of history. Only the reading of history can give one an understanding of mass movements, of progress and retrogression, of duration which outlasts groups of people and their institutions. All great questions of public affairs, as Mr. Truman recognized, are icebergs which extend far beneath the surface of current events. "Most of the problems a President has to face," he said, "have their roots in the past."

Mr. Truman's newspaper critics frequently spoke of him as an amateur historian. If he were amateur, it was only in the sense that he was not an armchair reader and writer of history. A man of action, he applied history as the engineer applies science. The writers of history, it is true, rarely make decisions. They are scholars, not men of action. But the actors on the stage of history whom they exalt and the real situations which they picture may encourage others to act.

The concreteness of past battles, for example, can inspire the discipline necessary for the struggle of life and death. The real disaster at Pearl Harbor inspired Mr. Truman to attempt the thankless task of unifying the Armed Forces. The specific example of Lincoln dismissing McClellan also encouraged him to do his onerous duty in recalling General MacArthur.

The concreteness of his historical knowledge kept Mr. Truman from relying upon easy generalizations. In corresponding with the former President I asked him what he thought he had learned from history that he could not have learned more quickly from the more generalized social studies such as economics and political science. To this question he replied: "My theory has always been that economics, sociology and political science are all based on history as it is made and as the biographies of men who have made history have recorded it. If these men and historians and biographies are not understood and remembered, history can not be used by the experts in a manner to advance the welfare of the world."

Mr. Truman's reliance upon the history of political campaigns saved him from being victimized in 1948 by George Gallup, Elmer Roper, and the other pollsters. Since the polls were showing the President's popularity at an all-time low, some of the Democratic leaders were becoming discouraged. But the polls did not daunt Mr. Truman. "I know," he said, "that the polls did not represent facts but mere speculation. And I have always placed my faith in known facts."

To offset the defeatism spread by the polls and to refute the misrepresentation of hostile newspapers, Mr. Truman resolved to take his policies directly to the people. Searching history for guidance, he found that President Andrew Johnson had "swung around the circle" between Washington and Chicago to obtain support for his plan of rehabilitating the South, a plan which had been fiercely opposed in Congress. He also studied Woodrow Wilson's crusade to sell the people on the League of Nations, a crusade which continued until Wilson's health broke under the strain. The examples of his predecessors were a clear warning against the hazards of the enterprise which he now contemplated. Nevertheless, he traveled across the country to the West Coast, making seventy-six speeches in the cities and towns along the way. As a result of his one-man campaign, he resored the optimism essential for political victory.

That he would eventually win the nomination as President, Mr. Truman never doubted. "Presidential control of the Convention," he said, "is a political principle which has not been violated in political history." It was a hot, humid night in July when Mr. Truman reached the Convention Hall in Philadelphia to accept the nomination. "Into this situation," he said, "as into every major experience which I went through in the High Office, I went with the consciousness of the history of American government and politics. The caucuses and conventions of the forty national elections which preceded that of 1948 were as real to me as the one before which I was about to make my appearance."

It was ten o'clock at night when he reached Convention Hall, but the lagging business of the Convention delayed his appearance for four hours. He waited patiently, almost gladly, not in a smoke-filled room, but alone on a balcony with a panorama of the historic city before him. The monument of William Penn, towering above the streets, and beyond that Independence Hall, aroused his patriotic sentiment and stimulated his thought about the political tradition in which he was now participating. "I seemed far removed from the turmoil and hubbub of the Convention within the crowded hall," he recalls in his *Memoirs*. "I let my mind run back, as I frequently do, over America's century and a half of political life. I reflected on the experiences of the thirty-one men who had preceded me in office and the campaigns which had loomed as large in their lives as this one did in mine."

From this rereading of American history, Mr. Truman drew the knowledge and inspiration which carried him through the hectic campaign of 1948. He gained moral conviction for the struggle by reminding himself that "throughout history those who have tried hardest to do the right thing have often been persecuted, misrepresented, or even assassinated, but eventually what they stood for has come to the top and been adopted by the people."

That a majority of the newspapers opposed him during his campaign for reelection did not dismay Mr. Truman. He dug into history and found that since Jefferson's election in 1800 there had been thirty-six Presidential campaigns and in half of these a majority of the newspapers had supported the losing candidate. This bit of knowledge kept him from worrying about the hostile newspapers.

The successful campaigns waged by Andrew Jackson also influenced Mr. Truman in his campaign in 1948. He thought Jackson had been successful because the people knew clearly what he stood for and what he was against. "One thing I always liked about Jackson," he said, "was that he brought basic issues into clear focus." His vivid image of a victorious hero enabled Mr. Truman to conduct a hard-hitting campaign and to put himself across as "the friend of the common people."

On a whistle-stop tour of the nation, Mr. Truman traveled 31,700 miles in thirty-five days and delivered 356 speeches, as many as sixteen in a single day. During this ordeal he never doubted his ultimate triumph, although his closest advisers were not optimistic about the outcome. The polls and a majority of the newspapers continued to predict his defeat up to the last minute. But relying upon the knowledge of previous campaigns, Mr. Truman was able to prove the polls so unreliable that they have never recovered their previous influence.

During his second term in the White House, Mr. Truman's greatest decision was the sending of troops to Korea to block Communist aggression. While he was at home in Independence, Missouri, for a weekend with his family, word reached him from the State Department that the North Koreans had invaded South Korea. This emergency obliged him to fly back to Washington. The flight of *The Independence* provided him the solitude for historical reflection. "I had time to think aboard the plane," he reminds us in his *Memoirs*. "In my generation this was not the first time the strong had attacked the weak. I recalled some earlier instances—Manchuria, Ethiopia, Austria. I remembered how each time that the democracies failed to act, it encouraged the aggressors to keep going ahead. Communism was acting in Korea just as Hitler, Mussolini and the Japanese had acted ten, fifteen and twenty years before." Haunted by the failures of the democracies to block the aggressions leading to the Second World War, Mr. Truman saw the decision which he was about to make as one that might prevent a third World War.

A constant reader of history while President, Mr. Truman has become a writer of history since leaving the White House. While writing his *Memoirs*, he carefully refrained from invoking hindsight to interpret his own career. "Any schoolboy's afterthought," he says in his preface, "is worth more than the forethought of the greatest statesman." Unwilling to exult in his own wisdom of hindsight, Mr. Truman has been impatient with those critics who censure him for not acting in 1945 with the knowledge that was only available ten years later.

As both a writer and reader of history, Mr. Truman has been harassed by the perplexing question of the role of the individual in history. In a recent letter to the author he said: "I am still searching, even at this late date, for the truth about the great men mentioned in the books left us by the historians. It is a difficult thing to do, but if science is defined as a methodical effort to find the facts, then history is the greatest of the sciences."

Whether history is science or art does not fall within the limits of this essay. But it is pertinent that Mr. Truman's curiosity about the past is as keen as ever and that his search for the meaning of great men in history goes on. It is pertinent, too, that his confidence in history as a faithful teacher has persisted. His remarkable testimony should inspire many to read more history, and it should be a perennial encouragement to those who have the difficult task of teaching the history of their own country and the world.

It remains only to summarize what history taught Mr. Truman and how it prepared him for the Presidency. It taught him to approach the Chief Executive's job with perspective, seeing it through the eyes of his predecessors and from the different angles of time and place. It taught him to read complex masses of materials quickly and imaginatively. History afforded him many precedents which stood as guideposts into the uncharted future. If the failures of other Presidents warned him again hasty decisions, their successes encouraged him to grapple with difficult problems. History also taught him to test generalizations by referring them to the concrete experiences of the past, and it gave him a sense of the duration of public affairs which prevented his seeking final answers to public questions. But more than this, history brought him fellowship with the great men of the past, and from this heritage he drew the courage and wisdom to make those decisions that have placed the nation and the free world in his debt.

DINOSAURS AND PERSONAL
FREEDOM / HARLAN CLEVELAND

IT HAS become the fashion in recent years to cry havoc about one particular evidence of social complexity—the weedlike growth of large-scale bureaucracies, public and private. It is true, of course, that a finer division of labor and the availability of economies of scale encourage the erection of unwieldy-looking pyramids of authority. It is true that governments get bigger, business firms and labor unions get bigger, newspapers become fewer, and huge organizations make a growing proportion of the decisions that affect the welfare and destiny of us all. But is it true, as much of the current literature would imply, that this trend puts our welfare and destiny in fewer and fewer hands? Does the individual have less choice or more?

My impression is that "large-scale" organization generally implies loose organization. Precisely because big organizations make most of the vital decisions affecting our destiny, more people are participating in those decisions than ever before. The number of decisions that *are* important to our individual lives is multiplying so rapidly that it takes a growing proportion of the nation's available leadership to get them made at all. The result of bigness is actually a diffusion of the decision-making and decision-influencing process far beyond the wildest dreams of those worshippers at the shrine of Louis Brandeis, who wanted to keep power diffused by keeping the units of society small.

In turn, the diffusion of power in such an interdependent society as ours means that each individual leader has more responsibility to his fellow-men than ever before. And so, as though in recompense for this added burden, the American executive leader finds he can exercise more freedom of choice than ever before—if he only learns how to operate within a large organization.

In an article titled "The Jungle of Hugeness" in the *Saturday Review* in 1958, Kenneth Boulding argues that things look bad for the individual in a world dominated by huge organizations, but cheerfully concludes that there is a good deal of room in the interstices *between* the behemoths, where "individualists . . . and people who positively like smallness of scale" can nevertheless survive. In the "Great Forest of society," the brontosaurus can do a lot of harm if he steps on you, but his feet don't take up much of the available acreage and there is plenty left over for the nimble and quick.

Everybody looks at the world through his own knothole; but Mr. Boulding and I must be examining different worlds. Throughout this article he seems to assume that large organizations are single units, hierarchical, monolithic, and forbidding; that the only position of power in an organization is the number one spot; and that the interstices of freedom in our society are *outside* the large organizations. None of these propositions seems to me to have merit.

Mr. Boulding's alarm stems from the observation that what he calls the Organizational Revolution is tending "toward ever greater degrees of hugeness. The electronic calculator, the punched card, operations research, and decision theory all point to a still further revolution in the making, to a still further removal of the scale barrier to the point, say, where General Motors (or the Pentagon, if by that time there is any distinction between the two) might absorb the *whole* American economy, and we would have, of course, a Communist State.

"The case for capitalism is the case for smallness of scale; the case for Communism is the case against the Brontosaurus—that beyond a certain point, increase in the scale of organization results in a breakdown of communication, in a lack of flexibility, in bureaucratic stagnation and insensitivity. There is a great deal of evidence to show that with present techniques of organization the scale barrier is reached long before we get to an organization the size of Soviet Russia, and that an attempt to organize a large economy as a one-firm state is doomed to inefficiency, corruption, and cruelty.

"At first sight, even in America, things look bad for the individual . . ."

Mr. Boulding is an economist, so I will have to assume that he has some evidence, not visible to my naked eyes, which persuades him that the successes of American capitalism are due to smallness of scale. But his general picture depends for its logic on an even stranger notion: that the only countervailing power that might affect, say, General Motors is power outside the General Motors Corporation. On the contrary, it is observable that very large organizations do not operate as single units with one commander in charge. Most of the checks and balances are internal to the system. The tensions within the system are many and so, therefore, are the opportunities for leadership.

In a household managed by people who can walk and talk, a baby begins to experience a sense of personal freedom when it masters the techniques of walking and talking. Just so, in a world dominated by large-scaleness, it is those individuals who learn to work with and in large-scale organizations who will have a rational basis for feeling free. There are, of course, plenty of free men who work for giant corporations or government agencies— but they aren't those who are so afraid of them that they scurry into the "interstices" of smallness. I have no doubt that a large number of middle-grade bureaucrats in the Soviet Union have so mastered the System that they are, in a sense, experiencing within its limits a significant measure of personal freedom. The reason is that the Soviet is not, as Mr. Boulding protests, a "one-firm state," but a myriad collection of organizations of manageable size bound together by leadership and a sense of destiny in ways not so fundamentally different from other nations as they (and we) like to assume.

Organizations *do* get bigger all the time. The Defense Department, whose growth so alarms Mr. Boulding, already employs 1,175,915 civilians (not to speak of soldiers, sailors, airmen and Marines) and uses nearly 10 per cent of our gross national prod-

uct. It spends more than the whole national product of Canada,
Japan, India, or Communist China, more than all states and local
governments in the United States, including all public education
for 40,000,000 people from kindergarten to state universities. As
my colleague Jay Westcott puts it, "Every other American institution or business is a dwarf by comparison with the Department of Defense. Defense assets are greater than the combined
wealth of the 100 largest corporations in America. (Indeed, some
of their wealth depends largely on their ability to get contracts
from the Defense Department.) Some individual defense instal-
lations have a greater worth than does the Ford Motor Company.
The annual purchases of the Air Force alone are larger in volume
than the output of America's greatest industrial producer—General Motors. The array of items purchased, distributed and used
for defense is forty times as numerous as those marketed by Sears
Roebuck and Company."

Do these facts mean the Defense Department is a dangerously
monolithic organization, that there is no freedom in its military
and civilian ranks, no interstices for individualists in the Pentagon
building? The President of the United States has had difficulties
trying to organize that Department's several satrapies under the
more effective control of the Secretary of Defense. The Defense
Department has never been a unit. The larger it gets, the less likely
it is to achieve effective unity. If it did achieve the monolithic
quality Mr. Boulding seems to fear, it would be dead on its feet.
It is the internal administrative tensions in a bureaucracy which
keep it alive. In this respect at least, a body politic is like the
nervous system of an animal.

"The bigger the organization," says Mr. Boulding, "the smaller
the proportion of its members who can really be at the top of the
hierarchy and participate in the major decisions, and the larger
the proportion who must carry out policies which are set higher
up." It is not clear to me that this is the nature of large-scale
organization. I would be more inclined to argue that a large and
powerful organization has so many more important decisions to
be made that there is proportionately more, not less, decision-
making authority to go around. The larger the organization and
the wider its reach, the more lateral contacts it has to make and

maintain, the more complexities must be sorted out by experts on complexity—which is to say leaders.

Moreover, in our society the larger the organization the more likely it is to be either a public agency or a private enterprise affected with the public interest. In such an organization the number of "major decisions" about *internal* management may simply rise in arithmetic ratio to size, but the decisions about *external* relationships, the consent-building decisions that are in the broadest sense of the term "political," surely rise in geometric ratio. It is observable that in a large organization affected with the public interest (a category which includes nearly all large business corporations and labor unions in our increasingly "mixed" economy), the nearer you get to the top of the hierarchy the fewer unreviewed decisions you make. The man who buys writing pads and pencils for a government agency is virtually his own boss, but the President of the United States has to operate in a world peopled with countervailing organizations in and out of government which believe his every move is of concern to them, and must therefore be cleared with them. The more countervailing organizations have to be consulted, the more members of the internal staff must be assigned to deal with them—and must therefore "participate in major decisions."

Finally, it is not true that in bigger organizations there is less room at the top. It may be that there is so little interesting "policy" to be made in some of the private corporations Mr. Boulding has studied that there is room for only one or two men to have the feeling they are "participating in major decisions." But a governmental agency wields such power that the lowliest field representative may legitimately feel that he is involved in major decisions. A junior field inspector of materiel for the Air Force may never participate in a "policy" conference with the Secretary of Defense, but his influence is great within his own sphere—and people judge themselves and are judged by others according to their influence (and their freedom of movement) within their own sphere. Doubtless, the local Communist Party hack in the U.S.S.R., even if he never sits in on a meeting of the Presidium, has an equally solid basis for high morale; he fixes his attention on the respects in which he is a big frog in a little pond, and chooses not to dwell on those aspects of his personal situation that would make him seem a tiny frog in the ocean of Soviet Communism. In spite of his unimpressive position on the totem pole of our agricultural bureaucracy, the county agricultural extension agent is a big man in his circle, disposing of substantial resources and representing, in the individual farmer's eyes, the power and weight of the U.S. Government.

I have known field missions of the U.S. foreign aid program in which virtually every employee had a vivid sense of importance, or "participation in major decisions," because the enterprise itself was palpably important and the daily work of each person obviously set precedents and could establish (or wreck) diplomatic relationships with a foreign power.

Mr. Boulding concludes that "small organizations, even down to the level of the 'independent person' will survive in the interstices between large-scale organizations." In our interdependent society one does not easily find the referent for the term "independent person"; but I suspect that those individuals will *feel* independent and self-confident who have learned how to survive and grow within large-scale organizations, not how to escape into the interstices *between* them. Perhaps Mr. Boulding should have carried his image of the brontosaurus one step further: If my son (our family's specialist on dinosaurs) is correctly informed, these huge beasts were remarkable, like the elephant, for their surprisingly soft tread.

It is a measure of the national mood that at the peak of American power we should be seized with the worry that large-scale organization is somehow a Bad Thing—that the very administrative skill which enabled us to build this strength and brought us free-world leadership is itself a threat to freedom.

My thesis here is the reverse: It is precisely by the development of his administrative skills that Man preserves and extends his freedom. The complexity of modern society and the omnipresence of large-scale organizations not only provide an opportunity for the fullest development of the responsible self; they actually place a premium on the exercise of a greater measure of personal responsibility by more people than ever before.

One of the results of modern technology and organization, for example, is to reduce the margins for error in a thousand ways. A hundred years ago most of the inhabitants of this continent were scattered about on farms or in rural towns with plenty of room to spare. But now that two-thirds of us live in urban areas, our accountability to each other is greatly enhanced. Childhood activities which used to be tolerated in rural societies are now regarded in cities as "deviant behavior"; one suspects it is not high-spirited youth that has changed, but the norms of delinquency against which juvenile conduct is measured. Similarly, for adults, driving a Buick on a crowded speedway requires more continuous exercise of a sense of responsibility to others than driving a Model T on a rural byway. A pilot of an air-transport has to make more split-second decisions, and is responsible for more lives, than the man who drove the stage coach.

All this makes life more dangerous, both for the decision-maker and for the rest of us who depend on his being right the first time. But do not these accretions of personal responsibility tend to increase the individuals' sense of personal freedom?

Perhaps the most dramatic contemporary example is that of an air-defense team watching for enemy invasions through the Distant Early Warning line. As warning of attack becomes a matter of hours (and in the future even of minutes), a heavy responsibility to all of us rests on the young men who will interpret the electronic smears on their radar screens. Unleashing our capacity for massive retaliation against an enemy is a fearful responsibility, yet the demands of technology have not concentrated this decision but diffused it to the far corners of the earth where a sleepy GI could cost us precious time—or an overzealous one cost us much more than that.

In many less stirring but equally relevant ways, the complexity of society makes us all vulnerable to irresponsible action by others. If a man wanted to shoot up his neighbor in the Kentucky mountains, the other residents could avoid participation in the feud, which might smoulder for generations as a "limited war" between two families. But a similar feud will not be tolerated by urban society. The interrelatedness of everything puts society's balance of power in the hands of the innocent bystander.

This increase in the extent to which each individual is personally responsible to others is most noticeable in a large bureaucracy. No one person "decides" anything; each "decision" of any importance is the product of an intricate process of brokerage involving individuals inside and outside the organization who feel some reason to be affected by the decision, or who have special knowledge to contribute to it. The more varied the organization's constituency, the more its decisions affect "the public," the more outside "veto-groups" will need to be taken into account. But even if no outside consultations were involved, sheer size would produce a complex process of decision. For a large organization is a deliberately created system of tensions into which each individual is expected to bring workways, veiwpoints, and outside relationships markedly different from those of his colleagues. It is the administrator's task to draw from these disparate forces the elements of wise action from day to day, consistent with the purposes of the organization as a whole.

Such a bureaucratic tension-system places a high premium on imagination, vigor, and qualities of personal leadership at all levels. The larger and more complex the organization, the more necessary it is for more of its members to learn and practice the art of building consent around a personal conviction—and reconciling it with the personal convictions of others. The finer is the division of labor required, the more important it is for the scientist or economist or other specialist to understand the process by which his expert judgments are stirred into the administrative stew.

The expert is no longer just responsible for "presenting all the alternatives" in a careful, scientific, and scholarly manner. He must also figure out who to present them to, and how, and what he wants to see happen after one of his "alternatives" is accepted. The expert is also responsible, in short, for being not only right but effective: for getting his thinking understood by non-specialists, and for carrying his recommendations to the point of action. In a world of large-scale organization, everybody is expected to understand and practice the art of administration. Those who do so effectively will experience a sense of freedom—not in the interstices, but right in the middle of things.

THE POLICYMAKER AND
THE INTELLECTUAL / *HENRY A. KISSINGER*

ANY OBSERVER of the American scene must be struck by the tentative quality of our policy both foreign and domestic. Major parts of the world are undergoing revolutionary upheaval; but we seem hardly aware that peoples abroad find increasingly little in America with which to identify themselves. Beyond any disagreement or dissatisfaction over specific policies there exists an ever-growing distrust or at least incomprehension of America's purposes.

It would be comforting to believe that this state of affairs is due to particular mistakes of policy that can be reversed more or less easily. Unfortunately the problem is more deep-seated. Our policymakers' lack of vigor is matched by that of many of their critics. It has been a long time since there has been a real debate on policy issues beyond a bland competition for slogans such as co-existence or flexibility.

This stagnation is often ascribed to the fact that our best people are not attracted into government service. But it may be pertinent to inquire how qualified our eminent men are for the task of policy-making in a revolutionary period. Others trace the cause of our difficulties to the lack of respect shown the intellectual by our society. However, a case could be made for the proposition that in some respects the intellectual has never been more in demand; that he makes such a relatively small contribution not because he is rejected but because his function is misunderstood. He is sought after enthusiastically but for the wrong reasons and in pursuit of the wrong purposes.

One of the paradoxes of an increasingly specialized, bureaucratized society is that the qualities rewarded in the rise to eminence are less and less the qualities required once eminence is reached. Specialization encourages administrative and technical skills, which are not necessarily related to the vision and creativity needed for leadership. The essence of good administration is coordination among the specialized functions of a bureaucracy. The task of the executive is to infuse and occasionally to transcend routine with purpose.

Yet while the head of an organization requires a different outlook from that of his administrative subordinates, he must generally be recruited from their ranks. Eminence thus is often reached for reasons and according to criteria which are irrelevant to the tasks which must be performed in the highest positions. Despite all personnel procedures and perhaps because of them, superior performance at the apex of an organization is frequently in the deepest sense accidental.

This problem, serious enough in the private sector, is even more complicated in government. In a society that has prided itself on its free-enterprise character, it is inevitable that the qualities which are most esteemed in civilian pursuits should also be generally rewarded by high public office. But very little in the experience that forms American leadership groups produces the combination of political acumen, conceptual skill, persuasive power, and administrative ability required for the highest positions of government.

Our executives are shaped by a style of life that inhibits reflectiveness. For one of the characteristics of a society based on specialization is the enormous work load of its top personnel. The smooth functioning of the administrative apparatus absorbs more energies than the definition of criteria on which decision is to be based. Issues are reduced to their simplest terms. Decision making is increasingly turned into a group effort. The executive's task is conceived as choosing among administrative proposals in the formulation of which he has no part and with the substance of which he is often unfamiliar. A premium is placed on "presentations" which take the least effort to grasp and which in practice usually mean oral "briefing." (This accounts for the emergence of the specialist in "briefings" who prepares charts, one-page summaries, etc.) In our society the policymaker is dependent to an increasing extent on his subordinates' conception of the essential elements of a problem.

The bureaucratization of our society reflects not only its inevitable specialization but also certain deep-seated philosophical attitudes all the more pervasive for rarely being made explicit. Two generations of Americans have been shaped by the pragmatic conviction that inadequate performance is somehow the result of a failure to properly understand an "objective" environment and that group effort is valuable in itself. The interaction of several minds is supposed to broaden the range of "experience," and "experience" is believed to be the ultimate source of knowledge.

Pragmatism, at least in its generally accepted forms, produces a tendency to identify a policy issue with the search for empirical data. It sees in consensus a test of validity; it distrusts individual effort or at least individual certitude and it tends to suppress personal judgment as "subjective."

The low valuation of personal views produces a greater concern with the collection of facts than with an interpretation of their significance; therefore the myth in our government that intelligence does not advise, it only reports. It leads to a multiplication of advisory staffs and a great reliance on study groups of all types. Each difficulty calls into being new panels which frequently act as if nothing had ever been done before, partly, at least, because the very existence of a problem is taken as an indication of the inadequacy of the previous advice.

The situation is compounded by the personal humility that is one of the most attractive American traits. Most Americans are convinced that no one is ever entirely "right," or, as the saying goes, that if there is disagreement each party is probably a little in error. The fear of dogmatism pervades the American scene. But the corollary of the tentativeness of most views is an incurable inward insecurity. Even very eminent people are reluctant to stand alone, and they see in concurrence one of their chief tests of validity.

Philosophical conviction and psychological bias thus combine to produce in and out of government a penchant for policymaking by committee. The obvious insurance against the possibility of error is to obtain as many opinions as possible. And unanimity is important, in that its absence is a standing reminder of the tentativeness of the course adopted. The committee approach to decision making is often less an organizational device than a spiritual necessity.

In this manner, policy is fragmented into a series of *ad hoc* decisions which make it difficult to achieve a sense of direction or even to profit from experience. Substantive problems are transformed into administrative ones. Innovation is subjected to "objective" tests which deprive it of spontaneity. "Policy planning" becomes the projection of familiar problems into the future. Momentum is confused with purpose. There is greater concern with how things are than with which things matter. The illusion is created that we can avoid recourse ot personal judgment and responsibility as the final determinant of policy.

The debilitating tendency of this approach is often obscured in the private sector of our society because the goals of our economic effort are relatively limited. They involve less the creation of a policy framework than successfully operating within one—itself a conciliatory procedure. But when the same method is applied to national policy, its limitations become dramatically apparent. Many of our policymakers begin their governmental careers with only superficial acquaintance with the problems of their office. This is partly because the rise to eminence has often absorbed most of their energies, partly because civic consciousness, where it exists, most often finds its outlet on the local level. Whatever the reason, few of our executives (or lawyers with business background) can benefit in government from the strong will which is often their outstanding trait and which gained them success. Consciously or not, our top policymakers often lack the assurance and the conceptual framework to impose a pattern on events or to impart a sense of direction to their administrative staffs. Their unfamiliarity with their subject matter reinforces their already strong tendency to identify a policy problem with an administrative breakdown and a policy solution with an aggregate of administrative proposals.

The impact on national policy is pernicious. Even our highest policy bodies, such as the National Security Council, are less concerned with developing over-all measures in terms of a well-understood national purpose than with adjusting the varying approaches of semi-autonomous departments. The elaborateness of the process is compounded by the tendency of advisers to advise; for silence may be taken to mean not that the idea under discussion is good but that the adviser is inadequate. The committee system is more concerned with co-ordination and adjustment than with purpose.

A policy dilemma is produced because the advantages and disadvantages of alternative measures appear fairly evenly balanced; otherwise there would be no need for discussion. (This leaves aside the question to what extent the committee procedure encourages a neutral personality to which the pros and cons of almost any course of action always seem fairly even and which therefore creates artificial dilemmas.) But in assessing these alternatives the risks always seem more certain than the opportunities. No one can ever prove that an opportunity existed, but failure to foresee a danger involves swift retribution. As a result, much of the committee procedure is designed to permit each participant or agency to register objections, and the system stresses avoidance of risk rather than boldness of conception.

Our method of arriving at decisions and the attitudes of our officials distort the essence of policy. Effective policy depends not only on the skill of individual moves but even more importantly on their relationship to each other. It requires a sense of proportion; a sense of style provides it with inner discipline. All these intangibles are negated where problems become isolated cases each of which is disposed of on its merits by experts in the special difficulties it involves. It is as if in commissioning a painting, a patron would ask one artist to draw the face, another the body, another the hands, and still another the feet, simply because each artist is particularly good in one category. Such a procedure in stressing the components would lose the meaning of the whole.

The result is a paradox: the more intense the search for certainty by means of administrative devices, the greater is the inward insecurity of the participants. The more they seek "objectivity," the more diffuse their efforts become. The insecurity of many of our policymakers sometimes leads to almost compulsive traits. Officials—and other executives as well—tend to work to the point of exhaustion as one indication that they have done all that could be asked. The insecurity of many of our policymakers sometimes is also shown by the fact that almost in direct proportion as advisory staffs multiply they are distrusted by those at the top. Officials increasingly feel the need for "outside"—and therefore unbiased—advice. Memoranda that are produced within the bureaucracy are taken less seriously than similar papers that are available to the general public. Crucial policy advice is increasingly requested from *ad hoc* committees of outside experts. (See, e.g., the Gaither Committee on national defense or the Draper Committee on economic assistance.)

These committees are often extraordinarily useful. They provide a fresh point of view. They can focus public discussion. They make possible the tapping of talent that would otherwise be unavailable, particularly in the scientific field. (A good case in point is James Killian's method of operation as science adviser to the President.) They may even galvanize the bureaucracy. Nevertheless they suffer from serious drawbacks. Whatever the previous experience of the members, they require extensive "briefing." This places an additional strain on the bureaucracy, while the members of the committee are frequently ready to make their best contribution at the point when the group is disbanded. Then again, the committee is inevitably drawn from the same segment of society as the top officials. Its members have therefore also been victims of the prevailing administrative pace. And the committee process, with its trend toward the fragmentation of policy and its bias toward simplified approaches, is almost as pervasive in *ad hoc* groups as in regular governmental committees.

In some respects *ad hoc* groups can even be said to represent an important diversion of talent. The number of outstanding individuals with experience in a given field is severely limited. As a result the same group is called again and again on related tasks. Its discussions soon become predictable and sometimes even stereotyped. The ideal situation would be a "leap-frogging" process in which the current high officials expend their intellectual capital while others, usually outside government, develop new concepts and approaches. But constant membership on committees causes many of their members to stagnate and freezes them at the level of the experience or effort that gained them their reputation.

Moreover, outside groups are handicapped by the fact that unless they constitute themselves into a pressure group seeking to mold public opinion—a function beyond their scope and usually contrary to their purpose—they can be effective only if they convince the bureaucracy. If they are too far in advance of existing thinking, they are ignored. If they only confirm what has already been considered within the government, they are unnecessary. *Ad hoc* committees generally can be effective only in a narrowly circumscribed area which may be somewhat ahead of official views but which rarely touches the essence of the problem: to challenge the existing assumptions or to define a new sense of direction.

The committee system not only has a tendency to ask the wrong questions, it also puts a premium on the wrong qualities. The committee process is geared to the pace of conversation. Even where the agenda is composed of memoranda, these are prepared primarily as a background for discussion, and they stand and fall on the skill with which they are presented. Hence quickness of comprehension is more important than reflectiveness, fluency more useful than creativeness. The ideal "committee man" does not make his associates uncomfortable; he does not operate with ideas too far outside of what is generally accepted. Thus the thrust of committees is toward a standard of average performance. Since a complicated idea cannot be easily absorbed by ear—particularly when it is new—committees lean toward what fits in with the most familiar experience of their members. They therefore produce great pressure in favor of the *status quo*. Committees are consumers and sometimes sterilizers of ideas, rarely creators of them.

For all their cumbersome procedure and their striving for "objectivity," there is something approaching frivolity about many committees. Ideas are accepted because no one can think of an objection fast enough; or they are rejected because they cannot readily be grasped. Unfortunately, not everything that sounds plausible is important and many important ideas do not seem plausible—at least at first glance, the only glance permitted by most committees. Rapidity of comprehension is not always equivalent to responsible assessment; it may even be contrary to it. The result is a vicious circle: in the absence of well-understood goals each problem becomes a special case. But the more fragmented our approach to policy, the more difficult it becomes to act consistently and purposefully. The typical pattern of our governmental process is therefore endless debate about whether a given set of circumstances is in fact a problem, until a crisis removes all doubts but also the possibility of effective action. The committee system, which is an attempt to reduce the inward insecurity of our top personnel, leads to the paradoxical consequence of institutionalizing it.

The result is that American policy displays a combination of abstractness and rigidity. Our method of arriving at decisions and the qualities it reflects and rewards place a greater premium on form than on substance. Thus on any given issue some paper will be produced for almost any eventuality. But because policy results from what are in effect adversary procedings, proposals by the various departments or agencies are often overstated to permit compromise, or phrased vaguely to allow freedom of interpretation. In any case, what is considered policy is usually the embodiment of a consensus in a paper. The very qualities which make the consensus possible tend to inhibit sustained and subtle effort: for the statement is frequently so general that it must be renegotiated when the situation to which it applies arises.

The rigidity of American policy is therefore a symptom of the psychological burden placed on our policymakers. Policies developed with great inward doubt become almost sacrosanct as soon as they are finally officially adopted. The reason is psychological. The *status quo* has at least the advantage of familiarity. An attempt to change course involves the prospect that the whole searing process of arriving at a decision will have to be repeated. By the same token, most of our initiatives tend to occur during crisis periods. When frustration becomes too great or a crisis brooks no further evasion, there arises the demand for innovation almost for its own sake. Yet innovation cannot be achieved by fiat. Crisis conditions do not encourage calm consideration; they rarely permit anything except defensive moves.

The combination of unreflectiveness produced by the style of life of our most eminent people in and out of government, faith in administrative processes, and the conversational approach to policy accounts for much of the uncertainty of our policy. It leads to an enormous waste of intellectual resources. The price we pay for the absence of a sense of direction is that we appear to the rest of the world as vacillating, confused, and, what is most worrisome, increasingly irrelevant.

In a revolutionary period, then, it is precisely the practical man who is most apt to become a prisoner of events. It is most frequently the administrator who is unable to transcend the requirements of the moment. Are there any groups in our society who can overcome this impasse? How about those who are not engaged in administrative tasks nor part of large organizations; the individuals who devote themselves to furthering or disseminating knowledge—the intellectuals?

Any survey of the contemporary American scene reveals, however, that the problem is more complicated than our refusal or inability to utilize this source of talent. Many organizations, governmental or private, rely on panels of experts. Political leaders have intellectuals as advisers. Throughout our society, policy-planning bodies proliferate. Research organizations multiply. The need for talent is a theme of countless reports. What then is the difficulty?

One problem is the demand for expertise itself. Every problem which our society becomes concerned about—leaving aside the question whether these are always the most significant—calls into being panels, committees, or study groups supported by either private or governmental funds. Many organizations constantly call on intellectuals. As a result, intellectuals with a reputation soon find themselves so burdened that their pace of life hardly differs from that of the executives whom they advise. They cannot supply perspective because they are as harassed as the policymakers. In his desire to be helpful, the intellectual is too frequently compelled to sacrifice what should be his greatest contribution to society: his creativity.

Moreover, the pressure is not only produced by the organizations that ask for advice: some of it is generated by the self-image of the intellectual. In a pragmatic society, it is almost inevitable not only that the pursuit of knowledge for its own sake should be lightly regarded by the community but also that it should engender feelings of insecurity or even guilt among some of those who have dedicated themselves to it. There are many who believe that their ultimate contribution as intellectuals depends on the degree of their participation in what is considered the active life. It is not a long step from the willingness to give advice to having one's self-esteem gratified by a consulting relationship with a large organization. And since individuals who challenge the presuppositions of the bureaucracy, governmental or private, rarely can keep their positions as advisers, great pressures are created to elaborate on familiar themes rather than risk new departures that may both fail and prove unacceptable.

The great valuation our society places on expertise may be even more inimical to innovation than indifference. Since the American intellectual is so strongly committed to the same pragmatic values as the rest of society, it produces a tremendous overspecialization. This in turn makes it difficult for the intellectual to introduce a general perspective even from the vantage point of his own calling. Panels of experts are deliberately assembled to contain representatives of particular approaches: a committee on military policy will have spokesmen for the "all-out war" as well as for the "limited war" concept. A committee on foreign policy will have proponents for the "uncommitted areas" as well as specialists for Europe. These are then expected to adjust their differences by analogy with the committee procedure of the bureaucracy. Not surprisingly, the result is more often a common denominator than a well-rounded point of view.

This tendency is compounded by the conception of the intellectual held by the officials or organizations that call on him. The specialization of functions of a bureaucratized society delimits tasks and establishes categories of expectations. A person is considered suitable for assignments within certain classifications. But the classification of the intellectual is determined by the premium our society places on administrative skill. The intellectual is rarely found at the level where decisions are made; his role is commonly advisory. He is called in as a "specialist" in ideas whose advice is compounded with that of others from different fields of endeavor on the assumption that the policymaker is able to choose the correct amalgam between "theoretical" and "practical" advice. And even in this capacity the intellectual is not a free agent. It is the executive who determines in the first place whether he needs advice. He and the bureaucracy frame the question to be answered. The policymaker determines the standard of relevance. He decides who is consulted and thereby the definition of "expertness."

The fact that the need for excellence is constantly invoked is no guarantee that its nature will be understood. Excellence is more often though to consist in the ability to perform the familiar as well as possible than in pushing back the frontiers of knowledge or insight. The search for talent consists more frequently in seeking personnel for well-understood task than in an effort to bring about an environment that constantly produces new and not yet imagined types of performance. The "expert" not uncommonly is the person who elaborates the existing framework most ably, rather than the individual charting new paths.

The contribution of the intellectual to policy is therefore in terms of criteria that he has played a minor role in establishing. He is rarely given the opportunity to point out that a query delimits a range of possible solutions or that an issue is posed in irrelevant terms. He is asked to solve problems, not to contribute to the definition of goals. Where decisions are arrived at by negotiation, the intellectual—particularly if he is not himself part of the bureaucracy—is a useful weight in the scale. He can serve as a means to filter ideas to the top outside of organization channels or as a legitimizer for the viewpoint of contending factions within and among departments. This is why many organizations build up batteries of outside experts or create semi-independent research groups, and why articles or books become tools in the bureaucratic struggle. In short, all too often what the policymaker wants from the intellectual is not ideas but endorsement.

This is not to say that the motivation of the policymaker toward the intellectual is cynical. The policymaker sincerely wants help. His problem is that he does not know the nature of the help he requires. And he generally does not become aware of a need until the problem is already critical. He is subject to the misconception that he can make an effective choice among conflicting advisers on the basis of administrative rules of thumb and without being fully familiar with the subject matter. Of necessity the bureaucracy gears the intellectual effort to its own requirements and its own pace: the deadlines are inevitably those of the policy-maker, and all too often they demand a premature disclosure of ideas which are then dissected before they are fully developed. The administrative approach to intellectual effort tends to destroy the environment from which innovation grows. Its insistence on "results" discourages the intellectual climate that might produce important ideas whether or not the bureaucracy feels it needs them.

For these reasons, research institutes set up by governmental agencies have sometimes reflected the views of their sponsor even when they were financially independent. As long as the sponsoring agency retains the right to define the tasks of its research agency —or even the majority of these tasks—it will also determine the point of view of the product. The uniformity of the administrative approach is after all primarily the result less of fiscal control than of all the intangibles of fellowship and concern produced by association with a particular group and constant concentration on the same range of issues. It is not overcome if the "outside" research institute has no greater possibility for applying a wider perspective than its sponsoring agency has.

Thus though the intellectual participates in policymaking to an almost unprecedented degree, the result has not necessarily been salutary for him or of full benefit for the organization using him. In fact, the two have sometimes compounded each other's weaknesses. Nor has the present manner of utilizing outside experts and research institutes done more than reduce somewhat the dilemmas of the policymakers. The production of so much research often simply adds another burden to already over-worked officials. It tends to divert attention from the act of judgment on which policy ultimately depends to the assembly of facts—which is relatively the easiest step in policy formation. Few if any of the recent crises of U.S. policy have been caused by the unavailability of data. Our policymakers do not lack advice; they are in many respects overwhelmed by it. They do lack criteria on which to base judgments. In the absence of commonly understood and meaningful standards, all advice tends to become equivalent. In seeking to help the bureaucracy out of this maze, the intellectual too frequently becomes an extension of the administrative machine, accepting its criteria and elaborating its problems. While this too is a necessary task and sometimes even an important one, it does not touch the heart of the problem: that purpose must dominate the mechanism if we are to avoid disaster. The dilemma of our policy is not so much that it cannot act on what it has defined as useful—though this too happens occasionally—but that the standards of utility are in need of redefinition. Neither the intellectual nor the policymaker performs his full responsibility if he shies away from this essential task.

This is not a call for the intellectual to remain aloof from policymaking. Nor have intellectuals who have chosen withdrawal necessarily helped the situation. There are intellectuals outside the bureaucracy who are not part of the maelstrom of committees and study groups but who have nevertheless contributed to the existing stagnation through a perfectionism that paralyzes action by posing unreal alternatives. (If we have the choice between rebuilding our cities or launching a satellite, we must choose the former.) There are intellectuals within the bureaucracy who have avoided the administrative approach but who must share the responsibility for the prevailing confusion because they refuse to recognize the inevitable element of conjecture in policymaking. (How can we be *sure* about Soviet motives? How can we be *certain* that in say thirty years the Soviet system will not be like ours?) The intellectuals of other countries in the free world where the influence of pragmatism is less pronounced and the demands of the bureaucracies less insatiable have not made a more significant contribution. The spiritual malaise described here may have other symptoms elsewhere. The fact remains that the entire free world suffers not only from administrative myopia but also from self-righteousness and the lack of a sense of direction.

One reason why intellectuals outside the administrative machines have not made a greater contribution is that for them protest has too often become an end in itself. Whether they have withdrawn by choice or because of the nature of their society, many intellectuals have confused the issues by simplifying them too greatly. They have refused to recognize that policymaking involves not only the clear conception of ideas but also the management of men. In the process analysis has been too often identified with policymaking.

But the equivalence is not absolute, particularly if analysis is conceived too rigidly. Effective policy fits its measures to circumstances. Analysis strives to eliminate the accidental; it seeks principles of general validity. The policymaker is faced with situations where at some point discussion will be overtaken by events, where to delay for the sake of refinement of thought may invite disaster. Analysis, by contrast, can and must always sacrifice time to clarity; it is not completed until all avenues of research have been explored. The difference between the mode of policy and the mode of analysis is therefore one of perspective. Policy looks toward the future; its pace its dictated by the need for decision in a finite time. Analysis assumes an accomplished act or a given set of factors; its pace is the pace of reflection.

The difficulty arises not from the analytic method but from the failure to relate it to the problems of the policymaker. The quest for certainty, essential for analysis, may be paralyzing when pushed to extremes wtih respect to policy. The search for universality, which has produced so much of the greatest intellectual effort, may lead to something close to dogmatism in national affairs. The result can be a tendency to recoil before the act of choosing among alternatives which is inseparable from policymaking, and to ignore the tragic aspect of policymaking which lies precisely in its unavoidable component of conjecture. There can come about a temptation to seek to combine the advantage of every course of action; to delay commitment until "all the facts are in," until, that is, the future has been reduced to an aspect of the past.

As a consequence, on many issues the short-run and manipulative approach of the bureaucracy and its adjuncts is opposed, if at all, by an abstract, dogmatic moralism that all too often cannot be related to the problem at hand. The technicians who act as if the cold war were its own purpose are confronted by others who sometimes talk as if the cold war could be ended by redefining the term. The Machiavellianism of short-term expedients much too frequently has as its sole antagonist a Utopianism that seems more concerned with registering a dissent than with contributing a sense of direction. The self-righteousness that sees in conscientious co-ordinating procedures a sufficient gauge of valid policy is little affected by a perfectionism that segments policy into cycles of domestic and foreign concerns (do we have the moral right to act abroad as long as there is a Little Rock?); or by a fastidiousness that spends more energy on establishing a moral equivalence between our attitudes and those of Communism than on defining the moral content of what we stand for. (Since we and the Communists distrust each other, an attempt on our part to claim superior morality is the most certain means to prevent a lasting peace.)

Thus if the intellectual is to deepen national policy he faces a delicate task. He must steer between the Scylla of letting the bureaucracy prescribe what is relevant or useful and the Charybdis of defining these criteria too abstractly. If he inclines too much toward the former, he will turn into a promoter of technical remedies; if he chooses the latter, he will run the risks of confusing dogmatism with morality and of courting martyrdom—of becoming, in short, as wrapped up in a cult of rejection as the activist is in a cult of success.

Where to draw the line between excessive commitment to the bureaucracy and paralyzing aloofness depends on so many intangibles of circumstance and personality that it is difficult to generalize. Perhaps the matter can be stated as follows: one of the challenges of the contemporary situation is to demonstrate the overwhelming importance of purpose over technique. The intellectual should therefore not refuse to participate in policymaking, for to do so would confirm the administrative stagnation. But in co-operating, the intellectual has two loyalties: to the organization that employs him as well as to values which transcend the bureaucratic framework and which provide his basic motivation. It is important for him to remember that one of his contributions to the administrative process is his independence, and that one of his tasks is to seek to prevent unthinking routine from becoming an end in itself.

The intellectual must therefore decide not only whether to

participate in the administrative process but also in what capacity: whether as an intellectual or as an administrator. If he assumes the former role, it is essential for him to retain the freedom to deal with the policymaker from a position of independence, and to reserve the right to assess the policymaker's demands in terms of his own standards. Paradoxically, this may turn out to be also most helpful to the policymaker. For the greater the bureaucratization and the more eminent the policymaker, the more difficult it is to obtain advice in which substantive considerations are not submerged by or at least identified with organizational requirements.

Such an attitude requires an occasional separation from administraition. In all humility, the intellectual must guard his distinctive and in this particular context most crucial qualities: the pursuit of knowledge rather than of administrative ends, the perspective supplied by a non-technical vantage point. It is therefore essential for him to return from time to time to his library or his laboratory to "recharge his batteries." If he fails to do this he will turn into an administrator, distinguished from some of his colleagues only by having been recruited from the intellectual community. Such a relationship does not preclude a major contribution. But it will then have to be in terms of the organization's criteria, which can be changed from within only by those in the most pre-eminent positions.

Ultimately the problem is not the intellectual's alone or even primarily. There is no substitute for greater insight on the part of our executives, in or out of government. Advice cannot replace knowledge. Neither Churchill nor Lincoln nor Roosevelt was the product of a staff. As long as our executives conceive their special skill to be a kind of intuitive ability to choose among conflicting advice and as long as they see this skill largely in administrative or psychological but not substantive terms, their relationship with the intellectual will produce frustration as often as mutual support. The executive, while making a ritual of consulting the intellectual, will consider him hopelessly abstract or judge him by his suitability in achieving short-term ends. And the intellectual, while participating in the policymaking process, will always have the feeling that he never had a chance to present the most important considerations. The executives' lack of understanding of the process of reflection and the fragmented nature of their approach to policy causes them to place a premium on qualities in intellectuals which they can most easily duplicate in their own organization. It leads them to apply administrative criteria to the problems of creativity, thereby making it difficult to transcend the standards of the moment. The intellectuals' unfamiliarity with the management of men makes them overlook the difficulty in the application of their maxims.

The solution is not to turn philosophers into kings or kings into philosophers. But it is essential that our leadership groups overcome the approach to national issues as an extracurricular activity that does not touch the core of their concerns. The future course of our society is not a matter to be charted administratively. The specialization of functions turns into a caricature when decision making and the pursuit of knowledge on which it is based are treated as completely separate activities, by either executives or intellectuals. Our society requires above all to overcome its current lassitude, to risk itself on new approaches in a situation different from our historical expectation. This sense of purpose cannot come from a bureaucracy, and it will not come from our present leadership groups if they continue to see the challenge primarily as a succession of technical problems.

It is true that many of the difficulties described here are due to qualities which also account for the strength and vitality of our society. Against the background of our sudden projection into world affairs we have undoubtedly performed creditably. Unfortunately, our period offers no prizes for having done reasonably well; it does not permit us to rest on historical comparison. Our sole measure is our ability to contribute a sense of direction in a world in turmoil.

The stakes could hardly be higher. The deepest cause of the inhumanity of our time is probably the pedantic application of administrative norms. Its symbol may well be the "commissar," the ideal type of bureaucrat, who condemns thousands without love and without hatred simply in pursuance of an abstract duty. But we would do ourselves an injustice if we ignored that the commissar is not just a Soviet but a universal phenomenon—the Soviet system has simply encouraged it in its most extreme form. He is the administrator whose world is defined by regulations in whose making he had no part, and whose substance does not concern him, to whom reality is exhausted by the organization in which he finds himself. Our challenge is to rescue the individual from this process; to escape from the pretentiousness and stultifying quality of an atmosphere in which all sense of reverence for the unique is lost in the quest for reducing everything to manipulable quantities. The way we face this challenge will be the ultimate test of our long-proclaimed belief in the dignity of the individual.

LEARNING UNDER LAW / *SCOTT BUCHANAN*

TO A TEACHER who has been led by training and experience to a concern about the whole educational enterprise, the current popular and professional attempts to reconsider it are alarming. They fall so far short of the extent and depth of the trouble as to raise the questions of the philosophers of history who warn us that we may have passed the point of recovery in the career of our civilization. Long and expensive researches tell us that we need more money, more classrooms, and more teachers; that the community must respect the teacher and the intellectual; that we must cut out the frills, and get back to fundamentals; that we should consolidate schools and pay more attention to the brighter students; that we must educate leaders; that we should or should not imitate Russia. These superficial criticisms and proposals rise from a deeper uncertainty and concern about our society. They raise questions of another order.

I should like to explore one of these questions. Before we, as a society moving into a new era, decide what our formal educational system should be, we ought to find out what educational processes and products our society provides in the course of its inevitable, natural, day-to-day life. This involves trying to see our society and its several institutions as an educational system; it involves the individual in seeing his own life as an educational enterprise. This is not the usual, nor perhaps even a fair, way to look at and judge a society or the individual. But in the absence of conditions for a controlled experiment, it may provide a perspective within which we can see the root or source of the educational energy which any deliberate formal system will have to tap, or adapt itself to, if it is to live, survive, and perform its functions. If a society has no built-in self-educative process, it would seem unlikely that it could by merely taking thought add or maintain any genuine educational establishment. If we should find that our society has lost its organic educational momentum beyond recall, this fact would be a portent bearing on our fate as a civilization. In spite of present evidence, such a sweeping negative finding is unlikely. If we are bold and shrewd in our search, we may not only rediscover the original source of our self-education but also haply uncover an educational process that has been growing and generating new forms while we have slept.

I should like to try to initiate such a search by constructing a probing hypothesis. It begins with an insight that was held in the center of the political thought of the Greek city state, namely that self-government is a self-educative process. We do not have to push this to the Platonic extreme of despair and say that there is no hope for a polity unless kings or citizens are philosophers. We can settle for the Aristotelian common sense that man is a rational animal, therefore a political animal, and therefore a learning animal. It was also common sense with the Greeks that the laws were the teachers, and that the making, obeying, and remaking of laws is the essence of collective self-education. To put it briefly, due process of law in any society is due process of education. I realize that this is an implausible hypothesis for us at present. We do not look at our laws and state in this perspective. Politics, in both its high and low meanings, is the enemy of education. But this antipathy may be the symptom, perhaps the cause, of our present blindness and paralysis.

With this hypothesis as a guiding principle I should like to examine our society for its capacities and facilities to learn. If I were a sociologist or a psychologist this examination would be the exploration of a labyrinth composed of rapidly changing and tangling ways of life. The labyrinth would also be haunted by the guarding monsters of law, political science, and history. For protection and guidance I would invite the authors of the Constitution and the Federalist Papers, de Tocqueville, and Montesquieu, adding what Montesquieu called the spirit of the laws to the formalities of jurisprudence. With such help I would like to see our free society formed by, or forming itself on, the laws by which we reluctantly or enthusiastically live.

The founding fathers all learned through their tutors what Montesquieu had said, that the principle of the republican form of government is political virtue, and that the source of such virtue is education. But, with the illustrious exceptions of Franklin and Jefferson, none of them devoted his attention and energies to the establishment of formal education. The evidence for their adherence to the principle is in what they built into the constitutions and laws of the new nation. They did their best to give this country the basic and comprehensive legal structure that would make the day-to-day life and work of the citizen and the officials self-educative.

It should be recalled at the start that the founding fathers did not invent *de novo* much of the legal structure that they built. The governments of the colonies came from England with the colonists and their corporate sponsors. The seeds of law thus imported suffered a sea change, and their transplanting in many cases made all the difference. The new soil and free air of the frontier worked miracles in the rejuvenation and in the forced growth of new meanings and effects of the old laws. But by the time of the writing of the state and federal constitutions, the imitation of the spirit and machinery of British justice and liberty had laid the basic pattern. As James Bryce has said, the authors of the Constitution were chiefly exercised in fitting a keystone in an almost completed structure, but this is not to underestimate the originality of the result.

COMMON LAW

But before we look at the machinery and spirit of the written Constitution and the legislated statutes, there is a massive and basic legal structure that was imported and taken for granted, the common law made by the accumulation of cases in British courts. The peculiar genius of this body of law and the story of its development over several centuries of vital human experience and learning has often enough been described and celebrated. Lay judges sitting by the side of the road or under an oak tree to hear, judge, and advise on their neighbors' feuds and causes, then calling juries to extend and refine their intelligences, early opinions being cited as precedents for judging new cases, such laws being tested and probed as much as the parties in conflict, the whole community remembering and anticipating judgment by peers as its members go about their daily business; we forget this fabric of our lives when, as we say, we avoid tangling with the law. Many of these lay judges became kings or the king's judges, many of the jurymen became legislators and magistrates, and the common law became the habits of the common man. It is the memory of this judicial transformation of needs, capacities, and conflicts into discovery, invention, rules, and habits that we imitate when we organize discussion classes in adult education and progressive schools. We have here a piece of the basic tradition of self-education in our society.

The facing of vital problems and the building of precedents by judges and juries flourished in the colonial and early national period of this country, so much so that de Tocqueville writes at some length on the extensive and prominent part that lawyers play in public life. The majority of the members of Congress were lawyers, but leaders in states and towns were also members of the Bar. They had been sensitized and alerted to the common good by their pleadings in court. Their basic professional training, then as now, was in reading and discussing books and cases under the several topics in the common law, property, contracts, torts, and crimes, as these had been sorted out and ordered. It is not so clear now as in de Tocqueville's day that the lawyer has the same sense of the common good, or that the citizen thinks about his part in the common life in terms of these topics in the common law. The subject matter has become professional and special, and the common man has lost one of the instruments of his political and social intelligence. It is questionable whether sociology and psychology can take the place of this instrument or whether the social studies, so-called, can go it alone without the legal formalities.

As has often been said, the reception of common law in this

country is as fateful as the reception of Roman law in Europe. Whatever the differences between Roman and common law may have been, there are special affinities between certain topics in the common law and another new discipline that shaped our minds and institutions, the discipline of the industrial revolution. When our national existence was being shaped, we were an undeveloped area, as we understand that phrase in connection with various new nations at present. The colonists came with the farmer's and the craftsman's skills, but very soon the curiosity and the inventiveness of the frontier combined with the new science and the mechanics of the old countries to refashion tools, to invent machines, and to set up shops. The War of Independence was fought partly to free such developments from British imperial restrictions. So again by the time of the founding fathers, technology, industry, and commerce had set the pattern for the industrial development of the country. Since this pattern involved new uses of property and new relations between men, the common law notions of property and contract were in for continual discussion and revision by both lawyer and citizen.

Without doubt, the industrial discipline, including those phases of it that we call technological, financial, and commercial, has been the most popular, the most fundamental, and the most effectual of our informal educational enterprises. We began in the colonies, and Thomas Jefferson still saw us as farmers and craftsmen, but the combination of the manual arts and skills with the machines and the mechanical arts began almost immediately. Yankee ingenuity and frontier resourcefulness welcomed machinery and organization. The instinct of workmanship was open to mechanical development and was free to take on organized efficiency as a virtue that magnified rather than restricted its capacities. Here, more than in the older countries, the new discipline struck deep into the mentalities of the people. The American farmer and craftsman had inherited a mythical, ritualistic, and superstitious relation with animals, plants, and even inanimate materials, but the machine steadily substituted matter-of-fact and pragmatic understandings even in the minds of those who still maintained the pious trusteeship and stewardship which the new Protestant orthodoxy imposed on the boss and his hired hands.

There was a great deal of learning in all this, and it took place in the pioneer's cabin, the frontier settlement, the New England village, the mill and the factory, and finally in the growing city. The learning resulted in the open, practical, relativistic, experimental mind, the mind that saw the use of tools and materials, the beauty of workmanship on a large scale, the infinite potentialities of the individual, and the multiplying effects of co-operation. The transcendentalist and the captain of industry might quarrel about the promise of the mousetrap, whether for a greater market or an oversoul, but they both started from the practical reality and utility of the gadget.

It has been and still is customary to attribute the relatively prosperous and peaceful course of the industrial revolution in this country to the guiding theory and ideal of free enterprise as it is expounded by Adam Smith. This economic interpretation of our history has been closely associated with, if not identified and confused with, the political doctrine of Jefferson that that government is best that governs least. We tell ourselves, at least at election time, that we must keep business out of government and government out of business if we are to keep our freedoms. Quite aside from the historical complications and controversies between and around these theses, there is a substantial and continuous bond between business and government in the common law of property and contracts. What an economist would call land and capital is called property in law; what an economist would call rent, interest, wages and profits would fall under the law of contract; and the founding fathers are at much pains to repeat with emphasis their basic premise that the essential purpose of government is to secure the rights and powers of property and to protect and enforce the obligations of contracts. This is something both less and more than writing free enterprise into the constitutions and laws; less, in that it does not prohibit government regulation of business, but, on the contrary, promises regulation by due process of law; more, in that it guarantees whatever the rights, powers, and obligations of men in their economic activities turn out to be. There are alternative dangers in this legal underwriting of the rights of property and the freedom of contracts, the conservative danger that Charles Beard found in the constitutional convention and its documents, and the radical populist danger in the executive and legislative powers to shift the weights of wealth and welfare under Jackson and others, both dangers contained in what Franklin Roosevelt called the elastic constitution. The founding fathers could not have foreseen the developments and their risks in the American industrial revolution, but they discerned, reformulated, and reinforced effectively and precisely those principles of the common law, property and contract, which have given and kept such order as we have in the commercial and industrial world. In these principles they found the essential minimal parts of the invisible hand that have identified the industrial system with the wealth of the nation.

But these bonds of obligation to commerce and industry that the government has accepted for the sake of the general welfare are curious and subtle things. Although the beginnings of commerce and industry in the colonial period could have been conceived, under mercantile principles, to be branches of the government, and although there are suspicions of the continuation of these ideas in the policies that Alexander Hamilton promoted, the emphasis on property and contracts minimizes and breaks any such connection. Such government action in behalf of the general welfare as there was, as in the cases of the Homestead Act and the railroads, distributes property to many individuals, who then manage to develop it by their own individual efforts or by contracts that they make with other individuals. The government does not force individual ownership but it encourages individual appropriation and defends titles in courts, and it defends, by enforcing contracts, any new uses of property that business and technology invent. Property in land, tools, and machines can be bought and sold freely; industry can be organized to exploit property by free contracts, and the government stands ready to justify and protect the rights and obligations so created.

It is these legal principles that put the floor of reasonable expectation under the structure of so-called free enterprise that has been built upon it. It must be this that free enterprisers refer to when they speak of the assurance of freedom in the Constitution, but they often overstate their case by claiming that the private conduct of business and industry is a natural and inalienable right which must not be interfered with by government. Of course, they add, government must put on the brakes when business goes to extremes, as in cut-throat competition, monopoly, conspiracy in restraint of trade, frauds or false advertising. This ambiguity, almost amounting to schizophrenia, indicates that the provisions of the common law which have been subsumed in the Constitution have been and still are being stretched to contain the continually changing realities in the industrial system. The New Deal was one of the crucial moments when this was realized, and the statutory remedies were hustled in to meet an emergency.

The common law in England has had two apparently divergent reputations. Its generation in the courts by the cumulation of precedents had at various occasions made it into a bulwark of political and social conservatism, rigid and inflexible. Its defence by great jurists at times seemed to give it predominant restraining power over both king and parliament. It seemed at these times that the common law was in principle incapable of adjusting itself to social change. It is this reputation that Charles Beard is invoking when he detects a bias to favor property in our Constitutional documents.

On the other hand, the common law has a reputation of pragmatic elasticity and reasonable flexibility, which has been celebrated in doctrines of legal fictions and judicial legislation. Novel cases stretch the meanings of the precedents under which they fall; they sometimes, more often than not, involve conflicting precedents taken from centuries of recorded judgments. Invention and construction of concepts are needed to make the law fit the case. The novelty that such invention and construction introduces into the meanings of the legal terms may seem to violate the strict canons of judicial procedure, and a rule of reason or even of social expediency has to be invoked to justify it. When the novelty is admitted it is often called a legal fiction; when it is incorporated in the judgment, it may be called judicial legislation; if it survives and becomes a precedent, it is from then on a permanent part of the body of law. This is the traditional way by which the law grows and adjusts itself to events and developments in society. It is reminiscent of the way customs survive by changing in an inarticulate society, but the legal formality brings it to a higher degree of rationality. In fact, it gives a nearer view of the process by which legal process becomes the self-teaching and learning process.

The American living and learning with the common law has always interested the British observer. British jurists only reluctantly accept the doctrines of legal fictions and judicial legislation, but the American frankness and enthusiasm in accepting and practising the doctrines have gotten British attention and even admiration. Part of the American ingenuity has been merely a readiness to accept necessary novelty. The settlement of a big empty continent, freedom from complicated customs, the ingenious filling of needs for new tools and machines have steadily eroded the traditional notions about property and have called for new kinds of mutual obligation under contracts. For a hundred and fifty years separate colonies went their separate ways in meeting different conditions in different regions under different forms of colonial government. This made it difficult to write and to ratify a federal constitution; or perhaps better, the federal was the only kind of constitution that could have been ratified. Private property and free contracts are like states rights applied to individuals. The government encourages each individual to govern his own property and to make the agreements under which he lives his social life, and it leads him to trust his own decisions by protecting and guaranteeing them. It assures to him a measure of self-government and imposes the responsibility on him of maintaining his freedom. Our government multiplies and distributes the power of decision to many individuals; to use Rousseau's dictum, it forces him to be free. The result is, of course, a fascinating and sometimes frightening web of ever-changing contracts and statuses, always passing away and coming to be, some falling behind and some jumping ahead of the needs of the whole society. This is the legal aspect of the cherished ideal of equal opportunity for rugged individuals. It accounts for the rootlessness and classlessness of our open society.

Ideally this kind of freedom presumes the equality of all parties in social arrangements, their voluntary, uncoerced, participation in making and keeping promises without fraud or deception. This means that the conveyance of property and the agreements for the use of property and for co-operation are made by deliberation and choice, not by accident and force. It is presumed that the points for the insertion of reason and will are widespread and frequent, and that proposals, bargaining, bickering, argument, and persuasion are everywhere and always welcome and effective. De Tocqueville noted that the spirit accompanying these habits amounted to a unique genius for voluntary association; sociologists note that we are a socially mobile people; and we all say with dogmatic defiance of immediate obstacles that this is a free country, isn't it? This is no doubt the authentic voice of the American common law.

CORPORATION LAW

But there is another consequence of the close association of property and contract in the common law. Property is owned and contracts are kept. The courts in fulfilling their duties to protect property and to enforce contracts continually remind the citizen of the mutal obligations that their freedoms imply. When property consists of tools and machines, and when contracts require relatively permanent associations, properties are combined and contracts are generalized. A new power emerges either by the accumulation of property and contracts around one individual or by the consent of many. In large and risky enterprises competition and daring may amount to conquest, and the enforcement of contracts may imply *imperium*. In a developing nation the government, speaking in a modulated mercantilist style, may wish to promote such enterprise for increasing the wealth of the nation. In consideration for this public advantage, the government in the guise of a contract grants a charter of immunity and privilege to a business and industrial company or to individuals who agree to organize such an enterprise. Thus out of a matrix of the common law and by a generative act of the government a new legal entity, a corporation, is born. The generative act is simple, but it is great with consequences. It binds together many generalized contracts into one bundle, which in effect becomes a bundle of laws, an estate, which is both a person who can make further contracts, and a private government which can enforce already made internal contracts.

The permanent structure of the corporation is composed of permanent general contracts, or by-laws governing the making, discharging and termination of other variable contracts, the whole facilitating the buying, hiring, sale and other conveyance of property, and enhancing the use of property. Thus, a legal structure and power is conferred on business, and this might seem to make the corporation an arm of government. But the notion of free and inviolable contracts is retained so that the government, far from using the corporation as its instrument or agent, is loathe to regulate it even in behalf of or in protection of the common good. Although the charters are granted by legislatures or by the executive, the government acts in the style of a court of common law merely to protect property or to enforce contracts as if the corporation were a natural person. Needless to say, this is not a stable, well-understood relationship. The government does regulate minimally, to maintain competition and to moderate extremes of power. Latterly, the government enters into contracts with the corporation as a party or person, but it is a moot question now whether these contracts are ordinary or treaties between sovereign governments through which the laws of the government increasingly become laws of the corporation, for example note the security regulations that accompany contracts for munitions.

The contract-making that is enabled by the charter is of various kinds: contracts with investors, contracts for raw materials, contracts with wholesale and retail companies, contracts with legal firms, the wage contracts, contracts with charitable organizations and with consumers. Some of these can be understood as contracts of one corporation with other corporations that are ostensibly peers or equals, but many of them are with individuals or obviously weaker and unequal parties. The latter kind of contracts increasingly strain the conception of free and equal contract. Power implies influence, and influence connotes coercion. In order to balance the inequality, the worker organizes a union to negotiate collective bargains leading to wage contracts; retail associations spring up to bring pressure in negotiations with big corporations. Even the big corporations make agreements or

cartels to divide the market and administer prices, to moderate if
not restrain competition. This would seem to indicate that the
contract that establishes a corporation is still a legal fiction, still
stretching the common law to cover somewhat incorrigible content, whose rate of change and growth does not abate. The business man and the industrial manager tend to see the corporation as
a dubious device for accounting and conducting their affairs, and
also as a trap set by the government which finds regulation more
and more necessary. The corporation invents ways of helping
the government in the difficult job of regulation, or it gets a
conscience with regard to its social responsibilities, or it wonders
if it shouldn't recognize further its status as private government
and imitate the public government by becoming self-governing
and accountable to its members. Public governments all over the
world increasingly appear as watch-dogs and policemen waiting
to take over and nationalize corporations that are not able to
discharge their public functions, or threaten to hurt rather than
help the wealth of the nation.

Although the internal legal structure and both the internal and
external operation of the corporation seem to be wholly constituted and guided by the common law provisions for property
and contract, and although the substance of the corporation seems
to the business man manufacture, buying and selling, the charter
and the seal are at least reminiscent of other corporate forms
that run back in European history through universities, guilds,
monasteries, and municipalities to the Roman family. All of these
held property and lived in the contracts they made, but most of
them had well-defined purposes for which the chartered powers
were granted, and to which the use of property and contracts
was more or less sharply restricted. Most of these purposes would
be recognized as contributions to general human welfare, not
mere survival and advantage of the members of the corporation.
They run to such matters as health, education, morals and religion,
and they imitate professional services. The business corporation
is chartered because it contributes to the common wealth of the
nation, but its legally stated purpose is restricted to private profit
only. Until recently, its board of directors could be sued if they
indulged in charity, or made corporate contributions to charity,

or to other corporations whose charters state charitable, not profit, purposes. The individual citizen is encouraged and protected in his pursiut of happiness by both seeking profit in business and by indulging in charity, but the business corporation, a kind of fictive citizen, must seek only profits. And the legal assignment of no purpose but profit seems to have struck deep into the internal habits of the corporations. The human relations inside the corporations have been until recently strictly business relations, for private profit only. The transactions are buying, selling, hiring, investing, and manufacturing. Courtesy, efficiency, and fair dealing to support these are welcome, but no nonsense about the firm being one big family, a team, a polity, or a society; and there used to be some distrust of executives and employees going in for these things in his free time on the grounds that they might involve a conflict of interest. Business is business, and when business in cases of hardship, calamity, or national emergency lent itself to charity and welfare temporarily, the interval was closed with the other slogan, "Business as Usual."

Over the long course of history it would seem that the granting of a charter created the presumption that the corporation and its activities were "touched with public interest," that its objective purpose, if not its deliberate and conscious intention, was to contribute to the general welfare and the common good. But the extension of the charter privilege to the business corporation would seem to call the presumption into question, or at any rate to minimize its importance. It is quite clear that the common-law insurance of property and contract is maintained to secure the individual in his private pursuits and that this is good for a certain degree of peace and order in society. It is not so clear that the strengthening of this security in the law of corporations serves the society as well. The testimony of the organization man himself seems to indicate that the private corporation is discovering that it is a team, a family, a polity, a society and that the welfare of its members, beyond the limits of business success, and the welfare of the surrounding and supporting society are its highest purpose. Corporation law no longer is restraining corporations from offering good-will in tangible forms for the purpose of creating a climate favorable to business, although the lawyers know that this involves a broad reading of the chartered purposes of the corporations.

Corporation theory would seem to be a central and complicated study in legal fictions, following the slow and cumulative developments in court cases, with very little help from statutory legislation. The corporation for centuries has been called a fictive person; it has for a shorter time been a fictive sovereign. The source of the first fiction seems to be in common law; the source of the latter in the legislative or executive charter. In certain conjunctions of circumstances and operations the corporation seems to be a veritable monarchy floating freely in a republican fluid. Various kinds of corporations, including the business corporation, have become governments or arms of governments. But all these aspects and appearances are only fictive interpretations and analogies with familiar traditional polities; they aid the courts in dealing with cases, and the lawyers in pleading cases. The fictions have not been assimilated to the body of either common or statutory law. They stimulate thought but do not substantially legitimize practice.

It is difficult to identify the educative function of the corporation, and to estimate its influence in our society. But some such attempt is being made inside the corporations themselves at present, and there is a growing body of serious study originating not only in Congressional Committees but in academic and foundation projects. Many leads are being followed, borrowed mainly from sociology and psychology, somewhat less from economics and political science. Andrew Hacker's paper, *Politics and the Corporation*, is a good example of the last, but it deals with learning as the process of forming opinion, rather than the making of political understanding. Perhaps a lead from Montesquieu's dictum will supplement Hacker's technical view: Virtue is the principle of republican government, and education is its source. Virtue in this context means political virtue in the citizen, not merely patriotism but an intelligent energetic concern for all parts of the common good; and education means not only acquisition of the moral and intellectual virtues in formal schools, but the continual cultivation and increase of these in civic life. Our question then becomes, what habits essential to a

self-governed polity are initiated and preserved and enhanced by
the citizen's membership in the business corporation? We have
seen that the private holding of property and the enjoyment of
its use through free contract-making under the common law
has not only developed the technological, industrial, and commercial system, but it has also emancipated and remade the
modern man's mind so that it moves rapidly, tolerantly, and
efficiently in the new matter-of-fact world. In addition to work
and skill the pragmatic world has enlisted general literacy, and
this has made possible the acquisition of reading, writing, and
arithmetic by more people than ever before. What has the integration of property and contracts into the corporation added?

Inside the firm itself, that is the manufacturing establishment,
the organization of business has more and more studied and
disciplined itself in the arts of management, the management of
men. The control of machines in a workshop entails the control
of men. There was a stage when the critical observer of this
development predicted that the machines would manage the men,
but the study and discipline of human nature has turned the tide;
men have learned to manage themselves as well as the machines.
And there have been at least two clear dimensions in this process
of the adjustment of men to the exigencies of the machines, at
worst making him fit as a bio-mechanical link in the production
line, at best multiplying his power and skill by the ratio that multiplies his handpower into horsepower, and that into ever-increas-
ing productivity. We need a new word, better than know-how,
for the educational result: handicraft has now been replaced by
machinocraft, the skills that make a man master of his functional
relation to the machine.

The other dimension of management involves the relation of
man to man on the job, horizontally as it were, and this requires
another vertical relation of workers to managers, shop stewards or
foremen, and the relation of managers to executives. Management
implies both technological adjustment and personnel adjustment. The corporation claims that it has initiated, trained, and
established a new profession—management; and that this is its
contribution to culture, not to say politics.

Whatever the effect of this so-called managerial revolution on

society as a whole may be, whether superficial or deep, whether
predominant or merely pervasive, the presence and power of the
pattern in the firm itself is real and decisive. The root of it is in
the original companies of simple ownership, where the boss ruled
the hired help. The professional manager has more subtle arts
than bossing, but these arts are limbs on the old stalk; in political
terms, the shift has been from monarchy to oligarchy, and the
managers are engineering or financial oligarchs. One of the subtle
arts would have it believed that the stockholders are an elective
constituency for the managers, and that they are highly functional because they hold the power of the purse. But this is so
extremely inaccurate in terms of voting and non-voting stock
and in terms of proxy voting that the argument about it ends in
almost proving that the relation between stockholder and company amounts to cancelling all the attributes of private property
except nominal ownership, a fiction that still directs the flow of
dividends, if and when the management declares them. The stockholder is pleased to let good management administer property
and contracts for him. The manager manages or manipulates the
so-called private rights and powers of the stockholder. The stockholder holds a ballot, can initiate a suit against directors, can sell
his stock, but none of these powers is understood or used as an
instrument of control. Tacitly but unanimously the power to
manage the business and to manipulate consent has been delegated
to the management.

Around the firm there is an environment of contractual associations, some of them organized as are the labor unions, some
of them like customers not organized, to bring bargaining pressure or to demand accountability. The degree to which the contractual relations are mediums of control and the degree to which
the corporate charter creates an imperial power over such
environments and confers a second-class membership on such associates is not a matter of clear definition either in law or in the
minds of the managers. The bundle of rights and privileges implicit in the corporate environment has not been sorted and
ordered explicitly; the common law cases that arise touch only
the single strands, not the fabric of the implicit organism. It is
only when the individual attends to the corporate fabric in which

he lives that he realizes the pervasive influence of the corporations in society as a whole.

It is now said that the process of deliberation that leads to the decisions of directors and managers could be carried on as well or better by the calculating machines. Highly elaborate data are prepared and submitted for consideration, and the combination of these emerges as the decision. The introduction of business machines is easy because the human beings have been habituated and accustomed to using their minds as if they were machines. It is not only the process of manufacture that are being automated, management is also automatic. This is obviously an extrapolation from current practice, and is no doubt exaggeration, but it is a suggestion, verifiable by other kinds of observation, of the kind and quality of the educative function of the body of corporation law and the practice that seems to flow from it.

CONSTITUTIONAL LAW

But perhaps we ought at this point to take a closer look at the processes by which law teaches those who make and obey it. The oldest and most popular jurisprudence has said that law is a rule or command of reason promulgated by an authority for the common good. A parody on this reads: A law is a command by the more powerful to coerce the weaker. American jurisprudence is famous for a more pragmatic view that laws are rules agreed to by the people to further their social purposes. No doubt each of these implies a recognizable theory and a method of education. But there is another dictum, that laws are questions asked by God, history, nature, or society to be answered by men individually and collectively. This formulation penetrates the heart of human freedom. It says that no law, not even divine law, cancels out human freedom; the answer can be Yes or No or something else. It also tacitly warns of consequences of the answer. But primarily it forces the human being to think about ends, or purposes. Law therefore provides a kind of complete Socratic teaching and learning so that under self-government men can teach themselves if they will learn to make good questioning laws.

Within this notion of law, corporation law has been and still is asking important questions. Its reticence about the purpose of the business corporation appears to be withholding an answer until it is found in the persons who so organize their activities. It is asking a big question about greed and the general welfare, about the citizen's concern for the common good. So far the answer has been incoherent and dark like the system of free enterprise itself and the various attempts to tame it. It may be that the question has been unanswerable as a whole until now; it may be that the integration of the technological system into one manageable thing, now imminent, has been the missing part that now makes the question intelligible. If the industrial, economic, and technological development of the country has been the implicit answer of the corporation for profit to the question concerning its purposes, this answer is now turning into another question, namely, what is that development for? Common law in property and contracts cannot give the answer to the questions that it has raised. We must look to the powers of the various constitutions in our federal system to see if they have raised, are now raising, or can raise the relevant questions for us to answer.

There is a curious ambiguity in the tradition of political thought in the West from Aristotle to the present. Aristotle says that "the state comes into existence, originating in the bare needs of life, and continuing in existence for the sake of the good life." This statement presumes that the state arose to meet the bare or minimum needs of human life, and that it normally goes on to discover ends and invent means for the sake of a maximum best of human life. It is not a complete state until it has done this. Historically something like this seems to have been the goal of ancient political as well as educational life. The long European experience in political life up to the seventeenth century seems to have found this goal illusory, therefore dangerous and vicious. For a century beginning with the British revolution and continuing through the French and American revolutions, there was a great political debate which seems to have concluded that that state is best that limits its aims to the "bare needs of life." The state that wishes to survive will not invest its energies in, or allow its responsibilities to extend to, the means and ends of the good life. There was not complete unanimity in this conclusion, but enough preponderance of opinion to last until our time.

It would seem that the American Constitution was written to keep the controversy alive, that is, to allow readings that will justify those who wish a minimal government and also those who wish a maximal government, or even a government within which both readings are combined to continue the theoretical and practical debate by checks and balances. The Constitution and the laws that are made pursuant to it keep a dialogue of questions and answers going. Government for us is a continuous dialectic about the means and ends of common life.

To some the system of checks and balances appears as an array of baffles to stop any impulsive and irrational power drive, a defense of conservatism. To others it is just the opposite, an incitement to agitation and the building of pressure and power blocs to balance the checks. To some it is just irritating or futile red tape. But what these see as a conspiracy has resulted from many considerations that lie deeper than any tactical advantage or disadvantage. One, and perhaps the deepest, of these would be the essential practical problem that goes with the fundamental theoretical problem of democracy. It had been said and believed that monarchy is the best form of government because the common good can become the general will of a people only through a single person, half prophet and half hero, perhaps chosen by God and accepted as king by the people, and clothed with office and its facilities. Legislation is a kind of soothsaying, not delegable to the many common men. When this office had been so often misused and turned into tyranny, and recourse had been had to the many common men, there had to be an alternative political process appropriate to the function. The interests, convictions, opinions, and reasons of many men had to be given due process by persuasion and deliberation. Otherwise no general will would be generated to approximate the common good. Persuasion and deliberation had to be formalized by devices, like Robert's *Rules of Order*, but also multiplied, disseminated and learned by the population. For this purpose, degrees and measures of local government would have had to be invented and set up if they had not already existed. And these essentially political units had to

retain or defend their degrees of independence. Therefore between the degrees and units of local government—town, county,
and state—there had to be checks and balances, and these
amounted to any individual falling under double, triple, and
quadruple sovereignties or jurisdictions. Even drafters of colonial
constitutions had to take account of the checks and balances that
these units entailed. Interest, opinion and conviction underwent
an ordeal by persuasion and deliberation concerning local matters,
but where local matters presupposed larger matters, representatives were chosen to belong to higher units where their opinions,
more or less informed by the lower local process, would in turn
be put through further trial by parliamentary persuasion and
deliberation. The representative was clothed with the formality
and immunity of office in order to clarify and protect the function. The deliberative body of the higher unit had to be restrained
from interfering with the merely local powers of the lower unit.
Here were more checks and balances, and the principle that later
became states rights; all powers not delegated to the higher authority are retained by the lower authority.

Geographical locality seems now to be too simple a principle
of the division of political work, but there was plausibility in it
in our early years because of the agricultural base and a comparatively homogeneous population. We have not kept up with
European re-examination of the proper divisions of a more complex society and economy, and their articulation within the
political process. Our inattention to political craftsmanship has
been overcompensated by sociological thought which has an
all-pervasive doctrine of radical social pluralism, which glories
in the co-existence of many self-styled independent social units
under a new brand of philosophical anarchism. This amounts to
the diversion of vital thought from the political process and hence
the unreality of much of our local and national politics.

But the geographical paradigm of political division and articulation, expanded as the country expanded, has been the base on
which the original constitutional and statutory structure was built,
and its quite remarkable functional success has borne out a principle that the Founding Fathers learned from Montesquieu.
Montesquieu had noted that large countries had been successfully

governed only by imperial monarchies, and that only small countries or cities had had successful republican governments. Given countries that had the proper basis in political virtue and in self-education, he had proposed that a republican government could be successful over a large area and population if it articulated its many and possibly diverse parts according to the federal principle. In essence this principle calls for the independence of the local units and their articulation by treaties between them that become also substantive components of their own internal laws. This, when carried out to its logical conclusion, means that sovereignty is divided, first as separate sovereignties distributed between the geographical units, as in local governments, and second between the local and the national governments with definite distinctions and powers to fit the specific functions of the lower units and general functions that belong properly to the higher units. The articulation of such a structure was, of course, the task of the Philadelphia Constitutional Convention; the Revolutionary War had already forced an attempt of this kind in the Articles of Confederation, which helped to define the problem. The resulting Constitution appears as a highly skilled job of making the distinctions between federal, state, and local functions. But it indicates that the authors were also aware that a developing country would generate new functions that would have to be sorted between local units and the federal levels. The power and procedure of amendment was provided for.

The Founding Fathers also learned another principle from Montesquieu, the division of powers. Montesquieu with his empirical roving eye had noted that when the legislative and executive powers are in the same official hands, there is a loss of liberty due to the consolidation of power. Laws confer powers of a general kind, which, if they are not interpreted by an intelligence that penetrates the concrete case and circumstance, become mechanical and tyrannical. Similarly, if the judges are merely the agents of the legislature or the executive and not independent and locally informed intelligences, there is loss of liberty and justice. He therefore laid it down for any government, monarchical or republican, that liberty required that there be a division and some degree of insulation between the legislative, executive, and judicial powers, and that these divisions should be pervasive throughout the governmental structure. Again the Constitution provides the model embodiment of this principle. In fact, because of these two principles, the federal and the division of powers, the Constitution is recognized all over the world as a model demonstration in political science.

But the purpose of the demonstration goes farther than these two principles of political science. "It has been frequently remarked that it seems to have been reserved to the people of this country, by their conduct and example, to decide the important question, whether or not societies are really capable of establishing good government from reflection and choice, or whether or not they are forever destined to depend for their political constitutions on accident and force." We shall not understand the system of checks and balances in the federal system and in the division of powers if we fail to see it as ordered to the end that Alexander Hamilton formulates in this statement. The system is elaborate and delicate for a high and difficult end. It should not be seen as merely a doctrinaire or ceremonial embroidery to give republican processes a hypocritical and merely formal majesty. As the source of republican government is education, so may federal republican government become the means of high human education. It took a very peculiar man to see in the gathering crisis of his time the farthest that we have seen in this direction. Fifty years after the writing and the ratification of the Constitution, Calhoun thought through the immediate problem before him and the country to what might have been the keystone of the arch, and his thought sharpens the divisions and the articulations of the whole governmental structure. That his interpretation and his proposals were not accepted should not justify us in neglecting his insight.

He was one of the first to see what we now see as power corrupting the reflection and choice of good government, and back of this corruption as its cause was not merely the industrial development, but also, politically more relevant, the dynamic tyranny of the majority. He saw the great dialectical process, by which opinion and interests were led and educated to express the general will and the common good, vitiated, interrupted, and destroyed by petty political machinery for getting a numerical majority to decide the issues of prosperity, peace, freedom, and justice. The political parties had already demonstrated that numerical majorities could be manufactured by accident and force, and their more subtle manipulations. The more educational processes of persuasion and deliberation could be by-passed and cancelled out by the machine and the steamroller, as they were later called. In many matters decision by majority vote still functioned as a handy *ad hoc* device and did no harm, but where power—either economic or political—was involved, as it was in the extreme in the issues that were leading to the Civil War, the danger to the republican political process was fatal.

Calhoun might have played, and possibly did play, the game of numerical majority, the numbers game in politics, but he also saw implied in the Constitution the rules for another better game, and he proposed that it be recognized and implemented. He called it the game of the concurrent majority. It called for a preliminary decision in the case of any issue whether it was to be decided by the numerical majority, or whether it should be decided by some political process that would come closer to unanimity, at least something that would assure that the minority interest and conviction would be included in the persuading and deciding process. It should be noted that minority opinions are sometimes minority opinions merely because they have been smashed or chiseled down to their minimal dimensions by nonpolitical processes. The procedure for Constitutional amendment took account of this and called for special treatment, including the increase in the required majority to something approaching unanimity.

Not getting much attention from those party politicians who were operating the machines that produced numerical majorities, Calhoun made the proposal that is now popularly associated with his name, without the context of reasons he gave for it. He proposed that the minority nullify the decisions of a numerical majority, if those decisions ignored vital convictions and interests. Such nullification would indeed call for disobedience of the law, but its aim would be reconsideration for concurrent majority decision. He asked for the formal recognition of such a right and the legitimizing of the procedure which would follow it.

The usual current criticism of Calhoun is that he was too intellectual, and this epithet is used as if it meant, like egghead, that he was not acquainted with political reality. He is also associated with the secession of the South, as an early instigator of that rebellion. His answer to such a charge would have been that the secession of the South was the political catastrophe which his proposal was framed to prevent. The spirit and principle of his proposal is nearer the principle of unanimity as it is practised by the Quakers. On unimportant matters the Quaker business meeting finds it easy to come to unanimous agreement, although the preceding discussion may show that not all members are equally convinced; but on important matters there is unanimous agreement not to make a decision as long as any "choose to object." There is here a concern about freedom of conscience and thought, but there is also a determination that both conscience and thought shall be informed and disciplined by common life and mutual persuasion. It is this logic that Calhoun was following, although he was not a Quaker. He wanted the government to maintain the educational process that he thought the Constitution protected, not only in its provisions for amendment but also by the federal principle and the division of powers. He wanted to see the formal recognition of the power of mutual veto between parts of the government commensurate with the issues that had to be weighed and decided by reflection and choice.

The reasoning that went into the determination of the elementary units and the superior parts of the body politic, is fragile and precarious, as most reasoning about liberty seems to be. Much of it was not new. But the authors of the Constitution emphasized and maximized the separateness and independence of the parts in a new and radical way. The Constitutional Convention probably would not have used the words "nullification," "negation," and "mutual veto" as Calhoun did, but Calhoun was following a logic inherent in their thought when he thus described the operations of the Constitutional provisions, and this is confirmed in the implied operations of the lower levels of government, as when the township even today objects to the encroachment of state laws on local prerogatives, or objects to any meddling by the selectmen in the affairs of the school committee. The division of powers is not merely the boundary line between jurisdictions; the doctrine of checks and balances created gaps between jurisdictions, gaps that could be closed only by the formal processes of mutual persuasion and resulting unanimous agreement, never by one-way edict or command.

Part of the motivation for making such gaps comes from the fear that the Founding Fathers had of elaborate and precise tables of organization through which kings had governed empires by dividing and ruling the provinces and the colonies. In these the precise articulations were mediums for the rapid and unchecked exercise of centralized power. The new American nation would need precise definition of its parts and their functions, but the danger of tyranny in such an organization could be checked and liberty protected by carefully placed valves and detours that would regularly run interest and will through channels of persuasion and deliberation. The gaps with their valves and channels would then be the points and loci where intelligence and wisdom could be engaged, and in turn where the public mind would be invoked and lifted to the level of the common good. The gaps in the legal system would mark the stages in the political process where the laws should be seen as questions put to officers and citizens for their considered answers.

An example would be a bill providing for a federal income tax. Government expenses have exceeded the income from tariffs, and some new tax source is sought. A bill comes before the House of Representatives, and a similar bill before the Senate. The House sends it to a committee for expert study or for hearings; it is brought back to the floor with revisions, and is debated there with special emphasis on its "political incidence," or in lowest terms, to see whether the congressman who votes for it and thus touches the pocketbooks of his constituents can be reelected. The parallel bill in the Senate is sent to committee where it is submitted to experts who will find out what the incidence of the income tax will be on the economy of the country, and it comes back to the floor where the possibility of the income tax being used as a power to destroy or aid business or to redistribute wealth is debated. The two bills are brought to votes in the respective chambers, and are passed, but with significant differences in the rates and scales and in the methods of filing returns and making collections. There is a conference between committees of the two chambers with new argument and substantial revisions, but final agreement. Then the bill goes to the President, where it is referred to the relevant departments of the executive branch. There is a veto and the bill is returned to the two houses and passed over the veto.

Then it is an act of Congress to be administered and enforced by the Executive branch through its relevant bureaus, presumably by the officials who had advised the President to veto it. The difficulties that had occasioned the veto now have to be dealt with by an operational interpretation of the act or the invention of executive machinery, and the reflection and choice of the executive branch and its parts are brought into effect. It is then channeled through the local agents of the executive department who by trial and error work out the details that fit.

Finally the taxpayer brings his judgment to bear on the fitness or unfitness of the law to his particular case and the anomalies are referred to the courts where the cases are pled before judges with or without juries. Difficult cases may be appealed and end up in the Supreme Court.

This hypothetical course for a federal measure has crossed many gaps where powers are specifically separated. It might have been stopped dead at any of several of the gaps; it has been stopped temporarily even in this comparatively smooth passage. The stops are made to allow, encourage, and in some cases to force an increment of reflection, a deepening of persuasion, and a public dialectic for informing and enlightening the citizen's as well as the official mind. It is possible that the issues and the causes thus generated will raise the level of discussion above the means and ends of the government to the level of constitutional amendment and even beyond that to the causes of civil war.

Actually we are of two minds as we watch and participate in processes of this kind. We like to think that the essential process is persuasion and reasonable deliberation, and that the gaps controlled by specified checks and balances are filled with the kind of reflection and choice that refine and weigh interest and opinion, and that the decisions are just and freely accepted. We are vaguely aware also that this process is a learning process by which we together and individually acquire and share knowledge of ourselves and the world.

But we also know that the gaps often appear to be vacuums into which chance, force, and organized interests are drawn before the reasonable process gains our attention. De Tocqueville discerned a national habit already formed in his time. He saw the democratic concern for private interest and opinion struggling to understand itself as a political factor, and he thought he saw the American solution in the processes by which minority opinion and interest built itself into a majority interest and opinion. The test of the validity of an opinion was its power to generate a majority approval and commitment to it. The American citizen came to believe very quickly under the democratic system that the common good consisted in private opinion getting itself rightly understood. We have had other illustrious expressions for this national trait, for instance, Justice Holmes's dictum that the validity of an idea is tested by its power to survive in the marketplace of opinion. De Tocqueville saw in this a powerful trend to conformity of thought and opinion. The pragmatists have often allowed the full test by practice to thin out into a social pragmatism which is almost identical with salesmanship and propaganda. An idea is true if it fits the prevailing set of ideas. This reduces persuasion and deliberation to the most superficial, quick processes by which a majority vote is achieved, and we have some familiar American expressions for this: log-rolling, passing the bacon, the steam roller.

These expressions imply something besides the propagation of ideas. They imply the accumulation and concentration of power of all kinds—personal, economic, psychological. Politics becomes the marketplace truly, where everything is up for sale, and let the best man and his interests win. Politics, in this style, becomes the making of "deals," and the man who has made the best deals finds it easy to make more deals, and the deals altogether build an organization or "machine." In a curious way, the political parties seem to have imitated the corporations. The "deal" is an informal privately enforced contract; money and personal favors are property; charm and prestige confer a kind of imitation of chartered authority; there is an inherent tendency to monopoly of politically effective opinion that generates power; membership in the party is a vaguely defined status, fictively determined by registration at the polls, actually defined by current operations such as getting out the vote at elections, or of distributing and receiving patronage in the form of appointive officers or privileges from the bureaus. Actual party policies, either those that are formulated as propaganda for party platforms and campaign speeches, or those that determine "deals," emanate from a very small minority manipulating goods, interests, and principles. The political parties are parapolitical governments combining in complicated ways a feudal and a democratic style, the latter now explicitly imitating the advertising methods of the big corporations.

It is these organizations that stand guard at all the "gaps" in the constitutional processes of government. Wherever reflection and choice are legitimately invited, some party agent or instrument stands ready and alert to inject power and privilege. We might get more efficient, perhaps not better, government if the political parties openly organized themselves in the manner of the Communist party in Russia, and accepted the full responsibility for using the constitutional processes for their own ends.

But there is a more incisive view of these matters. It would appear that the original constitutional provisions are not adequate to many of the quasi-political developments of our society. The industrial revolution introduced and still introduces technological systems and financial institutions that swell and burst through the old political forms; the corporations take over and set up their own parapolitical organizations. Professional men cultivate their activities and, when they become powerful enough, they seek legitimacy in associations. Similarly political parties have developed to fill what looks to the ordinary practical man like a vacuum of power and authority in the constituted government. Their legitimacy is only partly recognized by the government, and the power that is left over, or overflows, ramifies and grows without definite restraint. The result is that a dynamic society has split splinters off the block of sovereignty, and the government proper is surrounded by pseudo-sovereignties.

Each of these independent centers of decision, as the pluralists like to call them, takes on a peculiar kind of life. It is partly parasitical since it gets some authority by its charter or licensing power from the government, and its independence is such that it would not survive without its borrowed authority. But also, its operation takes on a piratical style; it intercepts the flow of the government's grants of privilege and patronage and distributes the resulting goods and services to its own clientele. In return it offers its expert advice and its facilities to the government bureaus. Each of these groups maintains offices in Washington and in the state capitols, and the national and state party organizations serve as clearing houses for this voluminous traffic.

The Greeks must have understood this parapolitical phenomenon. There is eloquent evidence that they did in Aristophanes' comedy, *The Birds*. The birds decide that they can accomplish their political destiny only if they set up their own kingdom, the kingdom of heaven, as they call it. They decide that their special skills and capacities will enable them to do this by setting up a barricade in the sky, a barricade between men and gods. They can thus intercept weather, trade in prayers and favors, and messages between heaven and earth. If they get into trouble in carrying out this plan, they can make terms with either gods or men against the third party and thus get a secure political status.

The comic elaboration and outcome of this plan need not concern us. But there is a speculative moral in it. The political parties have become relatively permanent artificial satellites in our political space. They have set up and manned barricades that screen whatever influences that emanate from heavenly or natural wisdom and filter into human reflection and choice. They mix the ideal residue of the screening process with whatever of interest and force they have in hand and feed it into the electoral, legislative, and executive receptacles through campaigns, hearings, lobbies. They confuse thought with propaganda and "deals" with consent, and use their contributions to assure reelection and perpetuate prestige, office, and power.

We like to distinguish our politics from European politics, and to point with pride to our avoidance of the extremes of many splinter parties or dictatorships. We explain the difference by our genius for getting on without doctrines, ideologies, in fact, without ideas. It is ironic that we should criticize their faithfulness to the rational techniques of government that are demonstrated in our Constitution, and that we should congratulate ourselves on our default in this respect. The European parties distinguish between ideas and interests, proceed to seek wisdom in various directions and from various sources, and then bring them to bear on the republican process. The truths they find are embarrassingly many and sometimes hard to face and bring to the point of decision. It may be that the problems and the realities that they reflect are many and hard to solve, but that the Europeans are learning more by a perverse intellectuality than we are by our anti-intellectualism.

SUMMARY

This paper began with a question and a hypothesis. The question was whether our society has in itself, quite apart from its institutions of learning proper, a principle and operation of self-education. The hypothesis was that law is such a principle, that law is the teaching principle in the self-educating process. The hypothesis helps to make the question definite and perhaps answerable. Within the narrow limits of my understanding, I have tried to make the question more definite by limiting my consideration to three kinds of law—the common law of property and contracts, corporation law, and constitutional law. These species of law are not exhaustive categories. They may not even be cardinal, the hinges upon which the body of law swings. In this short account, the omissions and the ramifications that have not been followed are many and weighty. But for what it is worth a summary must be made.

It would seem that the lively presence of the common law in a colonial country developing into a nation through the stages of the industrial revolution has been most important and consequential. Private property and free contracts enabled, guided, criticized, and legalized the industrial development of the country.

The law in regard to these matters raised through court procedures the questions of purpose and method that the citizens answered in the courts and in their day-to-day practical habits. These answers in their accumulation have become the unwritten charter of what we call free enterprise.

The habits and understandings which have evolved under this use and development of the common law are recognizable in the character and temperament of both the frontier and the great city. Spontaneous individualism and mutual aid, curiosity and inventiveness, matter-of-factness and experimentalism, pragmatic adventurousness and competition, equality and fair play, compromise and deals, self-reliance and compensation, a faith in the infinite potentialities of the individual and the unlimited progress of society, these are the moral and intellectual habits, the virtues and the vices, that make the American character. Their operation in the context of business and technology is ubiquitous and clearly recognized under the tutelage of the common law of property and contracts. The only reference to this basic law in the Constitution is in its laconic commitment to protect property and enforce contracts.

But the application of the common law to the steady and massive transformations of the industrial revolution stretched and transformed its meanings. From tools to machines and factories, from crafts to manufactures and machinofactures, from land and money to credit, these transitions mixed property and contracts and recombined them into new associations of men and organizations of both men and machines. Bundles of technology and law became organisms with lives of their own, and concentrations of power which the government had to recognize. Charters were conferred on them so that their power might be legitimate, so that private enterprise might serve the common good, or at least not damage it. The business corporations, thus generated from private property and free contracts, chartered and sealed by the government, had two natures. One of these, derived from the power to make contracts, made the corporation a fictive legal person. The other, "touched with public interest," made the corporation a private government. This offspring of business and government had a long independent but protected youth;

until recently it has not been required to respect and undertake its public obligations. Now it is showing signs of growing up and examining its accumulated powers and skills to fulfill its as yet undefined purposes. It is trying to discover the invisible thread that has from its birth tied it to the public welfare.

The corporate form again, as often in the past, is asking the questions of its members which may lead them to discover the purpose of their organization and incorporation. As yet it has had little help from government proper beyond an intermittent disciplinary regulation. Its members know that they have the industrial burden to carry for the society, and that its past education has developed the skills and organization for doing this; it has even developed the traditional skills of oligarchic government so useful in the management of affairs and the manipulation of opinion. It is quite sure now that these are parts or intimations of the common good. It is by no means certain that it will learn its next lesson; it is in great need of the laws that could bring it from adolescence to adulthood.

One of the reasons that the corporation is in danger of regressing to permanent adolescence is that the Constitution itself has a split personality. It was drafted by an extraordinary group of near-geniuses, who were ambitious to give this country an extraordinary government. Their aim was to transcend the analogies of political science that had accumulated in European history, the analogy of the machine, of the organism, of the natural family. They wished to fashion the government in the image of the mind, of their own well-endowed and well-trained minds. Representation, division of powers, and the federal principle are faculties of the human mind writ large. They seemed to assume that these faculties, once established, would develop themselves by proper exercise. For fifty years their expectations appear to have been justified. Persons like Justice Marshall in the judiciary, persons like Jefferson in the presidency, persons like Calhoun and Webster in the legislature sought out, discovered and expounded the implied powers of the Constitution, and by their practice of the powers they realized many purposes in the institutions that they built. It is in those years that this country became the teacher of jurisprudence and political science to the world, and the teaching is still going on.

But the Civil War was something like a tragic catastrophe. Politics had followed the rules and conducted the debates provided by the principles of the Constitution. Deep deliberation and heavy choices had been supported and carried out by the citizens and their agents in the government. The energies of freedom had developed power; power had concentrated as power does when it is blind; much of the fast-growing country had become colonial, not to European empires, but to the empire in its own country. This led to what has been called by Charles Beard the second American Revolution, and this became a Civil War. Force, violence, and terrible accident took the place of reflection, deliberation, and choice. The great tragic figure in this national drama was Abraham Lincoln, and the mystery of his ordeal still broods over the Constitution and its spirit.

James Bryce says in effect that the Civil War broke the backbone of our politics. Federalism provided a theory and a mechanism for defining and presenting the great questions of our society for the reflection and choice of the nation, its people and its magistrates; it failed properly to deal with the issues of the conflict that then became irrepressible, and the spirit of the federation died. This means that the delicate structure of the Constitution was put aside and new mechanisms were improvised to carry on public affairs. These mechanisms imitated the forms of common law which had adapted themselves to the energies and accidents of the industrial development of the country. Power and deals took the place of property and contracts, and the parties thus generated became the agents that used the constitutional forms for their own ends. Management of great and small affairs on both the national and local levels, and the manipulation of opinion by political rhetoric became the style of a new profession, the politician, and the electorate turned over its responsibility to the parties.

The constitutional structure had been devised to educate the public mind and to bring the citizen to the understanding and love of the common good. The education of the American community was to be through its politics, so that each man because he was learning to govern himself would become a better man than he could become by his own individual efforts. On the level of business and technology the common law has aided him to accomplish this. On the level of organization, corporation law has discovered and exploited new human capacities. But on the level of constitutional self-government there is confusion and frustration and a consequent regression to primitive political forms and to the mores of the marketplace.

But the story is not finished yet, and the questions that history and our legal system are now asking us to answer cannot be ignored or dodged.

NOTES ON THE CONTRIBUTORS

EMERY F. BACON, the Director of Education of the United Steelworkers of America, has played a leading role in labor education for many years.

SCOTT BUCHANAN is a trustee of the Foundation for World Government and a consultant for The Fund for the Republic. In 1956 he was a visiting lecturer at Princeton University's Christian Gauss Seminar.

HARLAN CLEVELAND, Dean of the Maxwell Graduate School of Citizenship and Public Affairs at Syracuse University, has held numerous government posts and has been executive editor and publisher of *The Reporter*.

HENRY STEELE COMMAGER, a prominent educator and frequent commentator on the American scene, is Professor of History and American Studies at Amherst College.

R. G. COWHERD is a member of the faculty of Lehigh University, Bethlehem, Pennsylvania.

ROBERT M. HUTCHINS, well-known as an educator and an author, is the President of The Fund for the Republic.

HENRY A. KISSINGER, the author of *Nuclear Weapons and Foreign Policy*, is active in both government and educational circles. He is currently Associate Director of the Center for International Affairs and Lecturer in Government at Harvard University.

ARNOLD H. MAREMONT is Chairman of the Board of the Allied Paper Corporation and President of Maremont Automotive

Products, Chicago, Illinois.

MARGARET MEAD, long famous as an anthropologist and author of *Coming of Age in Samoa* and *Male and Female*, is Adjunct Professor of Anthropology at Columbia University and Associate Curator of Ethnology, The American Museum of Natural History.

F. S. C. NORTHROP, Sterling Professor of Philosophy and Law at Yale University and the author of *The Meeting of East and West* and *The Logic of the Sciences and Humanities*.

ADLAI STEVENSON, a distinguished statesman and author, and former Governor of Illinois, has affiliated himself with many philanthropic and educational organizations. His most recent book is *Putting First Things First*.

LEO STRAUSS has contributed to the field of education as both a teacher and an author. He is Professor of Political Philosophy at the University of Chicago.

CHARLES P. TAFT has held several government posts and in 1947–1948 was the President of the Federal Council of the Churches of Christ in America. He is the mayor of Cincinnati.

HENRY M. WRISTON takes an active interest in American foreign and domestic affairs. An author and a teacher, he is President Emeritus of Brown University and President of The Council on Foreign Relations.